Lach And, Charmides

by

Plato

Classic Books International

TABLE OF CONTENTS

LACHES

INTRODUCTION.

Lysimachus, the son of Aristides the Just, and Melesias, the son of the elder Thucydides, two aged men who live together, are desirous of educating their sons in the best manner. Their own education, as often happens with the sons of great men, has been neglected; and they are resolved that their children shall have more care taken of them, than they received themselves at the hands of their fathers.

At their request, Nicias and Laches have accompanied them to see a man named Stesilaus fighting in heavy armour. The two fathers ask the two generals what they think of this exhibition, and whether they would advise that their sons should acquire the accomplishment. Nicias and Laches are quite willing to give their opinion; but they suggest that Socrates should be invited to take part in the consultation. He is a stranger to Lysimachus, but is afterwards recognised as the son of his old friend Sophroniscus, with whom he never had a difference to the hour of his death. Socrates is also known to Nicias, to whom he had introduced the excellent Damon, musician and sophist, as a tutor for his son, and to Laches, who had witnessed his heroic behaviour at the battle of Delium (compare Symp.).

Socrates, as he is younger than either Nicias or Laches, prefers to wait until they have delivered their opinions, which they give in a characteristic manner. Nicias, the tactician, is very much in favour of the new art, which he describes as the gymnastics of war--useful when the ranks are formed, and still more useful when they are broken; creating a general interest in military studies, and greatly adding to the appearance of the soldier in the field. Laches, the blunt warrior, is of opinion that such an art is not knowledge, and cannot be of any value, because the Lacedaemonians, those great masters of arms, neglect it. His own experience in actual service has taught him that these pretenders are useless and ridiculous. This man Stesilaus has been seen by him on board ship making a very sorry exhibition of himself. The possession of the art will make the coward rash, and subject the courageous, if he chance to make a slip, to invidious remarks. And now let Socrates be taken into counsel. As they differ he must decide.

Socrates would rather not decide the question by a plurality of votes: in such a serious matter as the education of a friend's children, he would consult the one skilled person who has had masters, and has works to show as evidences of his skill. This is not himself; for he has never been able to pay the sophists for instructing him, and has never had the wit to do or discover anything. But Nicias and Laches are older and richer than he is: they have had teachers, and perhaps have made discoveries; and he would have trusted them entirely, if they had not been diametrically opposed.

Lysimachus here proposes to resign the argument into the hands of the younger part of the company, as he is old, and has a bad memory. He earnestly requests Socrates to remain;--in this showing, as Nicias says, how little he knows the man, who will certainly not go away until he has cross-examined the company about their past lives. Nicias has often submitted to this process; and Laches is quite willing to learn from Socrates, because his actions, in the true Dorian mode, correspond to his words.

Socrates proceeds: We might ask who are our teachers? But a better and more thorough way of examining the question will be to ask, 'What is Virtue?'--or rather, to restrict the enquiry to that part of virtue which is concerned with the use of weapons--'What is Courage?' Laches thinks that he knows this: (1) 'He is courageous who remains at his post.' But some nations fight flying, after the manner of Aeneas in Homer; or as the heavy-armed Spartans also did at the battle of Plataea. (2) Socrates wants a more general definition, not only of military courage, but of courage of all sorts, tried both amid pleasures and pains. Laches replies that this universal courage is endurance. But courage is a good thing, and mere endurance may be hurtful and injurious. Therefore (3) the element of intelligence must be added. But then again unintelligent endurance may often be more courageous than the intelligent, the bad than the good. How is this contradiction to be solved? Socrates and Laches are not set 'to the

Dorian mode' of words and actions; for their words are all confusion, although their actions are courageous. Still they must 'endure' in an argument about endurance. Laches is very willing, and is quite sure that he knows what courage is, if he could only tell.

Nicias is now appealed to; and in reply he offers a definition which he has heard from Socrates himself, to the effect that (1) 'Courage is intelligence.' Laches derides this; and Socrates enquires, 'What sort of intelligence?' to which Nicias replies, 'Intelligence of things terrible.' 'But every man knows the things to be dreaded in his own art.' 'No they do not. They may predict results, but cannot tell whether they are really terrible; only the courageous man can tell that.' Laches draws the inference that the courageous man is either a soothsayer or a god.

Again, (2) in Nicias' way of speaking, the term 'courageous' must be denied to animals or children, because they do not know the danger. Against this inversion of the ordinary use of language Laches reclaims, but is in some degree mollified by a compliment to his own courage. Still, he does not like to see an Athenian statesman and general descending to sophistries of this sort. Socrates resumes the argument. Courage has been defined to be intelligence or knowledge of the terrible; and courage is not all virtue, but only one of the virtues. The terrible is in the future, and therefore the knowledge of the terrible is a knowledge of the future. But there can be no knowledge of future good or evil separated from a knowledge of the good and evil of the past or present; that is to say, of all good and evil. Courage, therefore, is the knowledge of good and evil generally. But he who has the knowledge of good and evil generally, must not only have courage, but also temperance, justice, and every other virtue. Thus, a single virtue would be the same as all virtues (compare Protagoras). And after all the two generals, and Socrates, the hero of Delium, are still in ignorance of the nature of courage. They must go to school again, boys, old men and all.

Some points of resemblance, and some points of difference, appear in the Laches when compared with the Charmides and Lysis. There is less of poetical and simple beauty, and more of dramatic interest and power. They are richer in the externals of the scene; the Laches has more play and development of character. In the Lysis and Charmides the youths are the central figures, and frequent allusions are made to the place of meeting, which is a palaestra. Here the place of meeting, which is also a palaestra, is quite forgotten, and the boys play a subordinate part. The seance is of old and elder men, of whom Socrates is the youngest.

First is the aged Lysimachus, who may be compared with Cephalus in the Republic, and, like him, withdraws from the argument. Melesias, who is only his shadow, also subsides into silence. Both of them, by their own confession, have been ill-educated, as is further shown by the circumstance that Lysimachus, the friend of Sophroniscus, has never heard of the fame of Socrates, his son; they belong to different circles. In the Meno their want of education in all but the arts of riding and wrestling is adduced as a proof that virtue cannot be taught. The recognition of Socrates by Lysimachus is extremely graceful; and his military exploits naturally connect him with the two generals, of whom one has witnessed them. The characters of Nicias and Laches are indicated by their opinions on the exhibition of the man fighting in heavy armour. The more enlightened Nicias is quite ready to accept the new art, which Laches treats with ridicule, seeming to think that this, or any other military question, may be settled by asking, 'What do the Lacedaemonians say?' The one is the thoughtful general, willing to avail himself of any discovery in the art of war (Aristoph. Aves); the other is the practical man, who relies on his own experience, and is the enemy of innovation; he can act but cannot speak, and is apt to lose his temper. It is to be noted that one of them is supposed to be a hearer of Socrates; the other is only acquainted with his actions. Laches is the admirer of the Dorian mode; and into his mouth the remark is put that there are some persons who, having never been taught, are better than those who have. Like a novice in the art of disputation, he is delighted with the hits of Socrates; and is disposed to be angry with the refinements of Nicias.

In the discussion of the main thesis of the Dialogue--
'What is Courage?' the antagonism of the two characters is
still more clearly brought out; and in this, as in the prelimi-
nary question, the truth is parted between them. Gradually,
and not without difficulty, Laches is made to pass on from
the more popular to the more philosophical; it has never occurred to him that there was any other courage than that of
the soldier; and only by an effort of the mind can he frame
a general notion at all. No sooner has this general notion
been formed than it evanesces before the dialectic of Socrates; and Nicias appears from the other side with the Socratic
doctrine, that courage is knowledge. This is explained to
mean knowledge of things terrible in the future. But Socrates denies that the knowledge of the future is separable from
that of the past and present; in other words, true knowledge
is not that of the soothsayer but of the philosopher. And
all knowledge will thus be equivalent to all virtue--a position which elsewhere Socrates is not unwilling to admit, but
which will not assist us in distinguishing the nature of courage. In this part of the Dialogue the contrast between the
mode of cross-examination which is practised by Laches and
by Socrates, and also the manner in which the definition of
Laches is made to approximate to that of Nicias, are worthy
of attention.

Thus, with some intimation of the connexion and unity
of virtue and knowledge, we arrive at no distinct result. The
two aspects of courage are never harmonized. The knowledge which in the Protagoras is explained as the faculty of
estimating pleasures and pains is here lost in an unmeaning
and transcendental conception. Yet several true intimations
of the nature of courage are allowed to appear: (1) That courage is moral as well as physical: (2) That true courage is in-
separable from knowledge, and yet (3) is based on a natural
instinct. Laches exhibits one aspect of courage; Nicias the
other. The perfect image and harmony of both is only real-
ized in Socrates himself.

The Dialogue offers one among many examples of the

freedom with which Plato treats facts. For the scene must be supposed to have occurred between B.C. 424, the year of the battle of Delium, and B.C. 418, the year of the battle of Mantinea, at which Laches fell. But if Socrates was more than seventy years of age at his trial in 399 (see Apology), he could not have been a young man at any time after the battle of Delium.

PERSONS OF THE DIALOGUE:

Lysimachus, son of Aristides.

Melesias, son of Thucydides.

Their sons. Nicias, Laches, Socrates.

LYSIMACHUS: You have seen the exhibition of the man fighting in armour, Nicias and Laches, but we did not tell you at the time the reason why my friend Melesias and I asked you to go with us and see him. I think that we may as well confess what this was, for we certainly ought not to have any reserve with you. The reason was, that we were intending to ask your advice. Some laugh at the very notion of advising others, and when they are asked will not say what they think. They guess at the wishes of the person who asks them, and answer according to his, and not according to their own, opinion. But as we know that you are good judges, and will say exactly what you think, we have taken you into our counsels. The matter about which I am making all this preface is as follows: Melesias and I have two sons; that is his son, and he is named Thucydides, after his grandfather; and this is mine, who is also called after his grandfather, Aristides. Now, we are resolved to take the greatest care of the youths, and not to let them run about as they like, which is too often the way with the young, when they are no longer children, but to begin at once and do the utmost that we can for them. And knowing you to have sons of your own, we thought that you were most likely to have attended to their training and improvement, and, if perchance you have not attended to them, we may remind you that you ought to have done so, and would invite you to assist us in the fulfilment of a common duty. I will tell you, Nicias and Laches, even at the risk of being tedious, how we came to think of this. Melesias and I live together, and our sons live with us; and now, as I was saying at first, we are going to confess to you. Both of us often talk to the lads about the many noble deeds which our own fathers did in war and peace--in the management of the allies, and in the administration of the city; but neither of us has any deeds of his own which he can show. The truth is that we are ashamed of this contrast being seen by them, and we blame our fathers for letting us be spoiled in the days of our youth, while they were occupied with the concerns of others; and we urge all this upon the lads, pointing out to them that they will not grow up to honour if they are rebellious and take no pains about themselves; but that if they take pains they may, perhaps, become worthy of the names which they bear. They, on their part, promise to comply with our wishes; and our care is to discover what studies or pursuits are likely to be most improving to them. Some one commended to us the art of fighting in armour, which he thought an excellent accomplishment for a young man to learn; and he praised the man whose exhibition you have seen, and told us to go and see him. And we determined that we would go, and get you to accompany us; and we were intending at the same time, if you did not object, to take counsel with you about the education of our sons. That is the matter which we wanted to talk over with you; and we hope that you will give us your opinion about this art of fighting in armour, and about any other studies or pursuits which may or may not be desirable for a young man to learn. Please to say whether you agree to our proposal.

NICIAS: As far as I am concerned, Lysimachus and Melesias, I applaud your purpose, and will gladly assist you; and I believe that you, Laches, will be equally glad.

LACHES: Certainly, Nicias; and I quite approve of the 180b remark which Lysimachus made about his own father and the father of Melesias, and which is applicable, not only to them, but to us, and to every one who is occupied with public affairs. As he says, such persons are too apt to be negligent and careless of their own children and their private concerns. There is much truth in that remark of yours, Lysimachus. But why, instead of consulting us, do you not consult our friend Socrates about the education of the youths? He is of the same deme with you, and is always passing his time in places where the youth have any noble study or pursuit, such as you are enquiring after. *Laches admires Socrates*

LYSIMACHUS: Why, Laches, has Socrates ever attended to matters of this sort?

LACHES: Certainly, Lysimachus.

NICIAS: That I have the means of knowing as well as Laches; for quite lately he supplied me with a teacher of music for my sons,--Damon, the disciple of Agathocles, who is a most accomplished man in every way, as well as a musician, and a companion of inestimable value for young men at their age.

LYSIMACHUS: Those who have reached my time of life, Socrates and Nicias and Laches, fall out of acquaintance with the young, because they are generally detained at home by old age; but you, O son of Sophroniscus, should let your fellow demesman have the benefit of any advice which you are able to give. Moreover I have a claim upon you as an old friend of your father; for I and he were always companions and friends, and to the hour of his death there never was a difference between us; and now it comes back to me, at the mention of your name, that I have heard these lads talking to one another at home, and often speaking of Socrates in terms of the highest praise; but I have never thought to ask them whether the son of Sophroniscus was the person whom they meant. Tell me, my boys, whether this is the Socrates of whom you have often spoken?

SON: Certainly, father, this is he.

LYSIMACHUS: I am delighted to hear, Socrates, that you maintain the name of your father, who was a most excellent man; and I further rejoice at the prospect of our family ties being renewed.

LACHES: Indeed, Lysimachus, you ought not to give him up; for I can assure you that I have seen him maintaining, not only his father's, but also his country's name. He was my companion in the retreat from Delium, and I can tell you that if others had only been like him, the honour of our country would have been upheld, and the great defeat would never have occurred.

LYSIMACHUS: That is very high praise which is accorded to you, Socrates, by faithful witnesses and for actions like those which they praise. Let me tell you the pleasure which I feel in hearing of your fame; and I hope that you will regard me as one of your warmest friends. You ought to have visited us long ago, and made yourself at home with us; but now, from this day forward, as we have at last found one another out, do as I say--come and make acquaintance with me, and with these young men, that I may continue your friend, as I was your father's. I shall expect you to do so, and shall venture at some future time to remind you of your duty. But what say you of the matter of which we were beginning to speak--the art of fighting in armour? Is that a practice in which the lads may be advantageously instructed?

SOCRATES: I will endeavour to advise you, Lysima- 181 d chus, as far as I can in this matter, and also in every way will comply with your wishes; but as I am younger and not so experienced, I think that I ought certainly to hear first what my elders have to say, and to learn of them, and if I have anything to add, then I may venture to give my opinion to them as well as to you. Suppose, Nicias, that one or other of you begin.

NICIAS: I have no objection, Socrates; and my opinion 181 e is that the acquirement of this art is in many ways useful to young men. It is an advantage to them that among the favourite amusements of their leisure hours they should have one which tends to improve and not to injure their bodily health. No gymnastics could be better or harder exercise; and this, and the art of riding, are of all arts most befitting to a freeman; for they only who are thus trained in the use of arms are the athletes of our military profession, trained in that on which the conflict turns. Moreover in actual battle, when you have to fight in a line with a number of others, such an acquirement will be of some use, and will be of the greatest whenever the ranks are broken and you have to fight singly, either in pursuit, when you are attacking some one who is defending himself, or in flight, when you have to defend yourself against an assailant. Certainly he who possessed the art could not meet with any harm at the hands of a single person, or perhaps of several; and in any case he would have a great advantage. Further, this sort of skill inclines a man to the love of other noble lessons; for every man who has learned how to fight in armour will desire to learn the proper arrangement of an army, which is the sequel of the lesson: and when he has learned this, and his ambition is once fired, he will go on to learn the complete art of the general. There is no difficulty in seeing that the knowledge and practice of other military arts will be honourable and valuable to a man; and this lesson may be the beginning of them. Let me add a further advantage, which is by no means a slight one,--that this science will make any man a great deal more valiant and self-possessed in the field. And I will not disdain to mention, what by some may be thought to be a small matter;--he will make a better appearance at the right time; that is to say, at the time when his appearance will strike terror into his enemies. My opinion then, Lysimachus, is, as I say, that the youths should be instructed in this art, and for the reasons which I have given. But Laches may take a different view; and I shall be very glad to hear what he has to say.

182e LACHES: I should not like to maintain, Nicias, that any kind of knowledge is not to be learned; for all knowledge appears to be a good: and if, as Nicias and as the teachers of the art affirm, this use of arms is really a species of knowledge, then it ought to be learned; but if not, and if those who profess to teach it are deceivers only; or if it be knowledge, but not of a valuable sort, then what is the use of learning it? I say this, because I think that if it had been really valuable, the Lacedaemonians, whose whole life is passed in finding out and practising the arts which give them an advantage over other nations in war, would have discovered this one. And even if they had not, still these professors of the art would certainly not have failed to discover that of all the Hellenes the Lacedaemonians have the greatest interest in such matters, and that a master of the art who was honoured among them would be sure to make his fortune among other nations, just as a tragic poet would who is honoured among ourselves; which is the reason why he who fancies that he can write a tragedy does not go about itinerating in the neighbouring states, but rushes hither straight, and exhibits at Athens; and this is natural. Whereas I perceive that these fighters in armour regard Lacedaemon as a sacred inviolable territory, which they do not touch with the point of their foot; but they make a circuit of the neighbouring states, and would rather exhibit to any others than to the Spartans; and particularly to those who would themselves acknowledge that they are by no means firstrate in the arts of war. Further, Lysimachus, I have encountered a good many of these gentlemen in actual service, and have taken their measure, which I can give you at once; for none of these masters of fence have ever been distinguished in war,--there has been a sort of fatality about them; while in all other arts the men of note have been always those who have practised the art, they appear to be a most unfortunate exception. For example, this very Stesilaus, whom you and I have just witnessed exhibiting in all that crowd and making such great professions of his powers, I have seen at another time making, in sober truth, an involuntary exhibition of himself, which was a far better spectacle. He was a marine on board a ship which struck a transport vessel, and was armed with a weapon, half spear, half scythe; the singularity of this weapon was worthy of the singularity of the man. To make a long story short, I will only tell you what happened to this notable invention of the scythe spear. He was fighting, and the scythe was caught in the rigging of the other ship, and stuck fast; and he tugged, but was unable to get his weapon free. The two ships were passing one another. He first ran along his own ship holding on to the spear; but as the other ship passed by and drew him after as he was holding on, he let the spear slip through his hand until he retained only the end of the handle. The people in the transport clapped their hands, and laughed at his ridiculous figure; and when some one threw a stone, which fell on the deck at his feet, and he quitted his hold of the scythe-spear, the crew of his own trireme also burst out laughing; they could not refrain when they beheld the weapon waving in the air, suspended from the transport. Now I do not deny that there may be something in such an art, as Nicias asserts, but I tell you my experience; and, as I said at first, whether this be an art of which the advantage is so slight, or not an art at all, but only an imposition, in either case such an acquirement is not worth having. For my opinion is, that if the professor of this art be a coward, he will be likely to become rash, and his character will be only more notorious; or if he be brave, and fail ever so little, other men will be on the watch, and he will be greatly traduced; for there is a jealousy of such pretenders; and unless a man be pre-eminent in valour, he cannot help being ridiculous, if he says that he has this sort of skill. Such is my judgment, Lysimachus, of the desirableness of this art; but, as I said at first, ask Socrates, and do not let him go until he has given you his opinion of the matter.

184d LYSIMACHUS: I am going to ask this favour of you, Socrates; as is the more necessary because the two councillors disagree, and some one is in a manner still needed who will decide between them. Had they agreed, no arbiter would have been required. But as Laches has voted one way and Nicias another, I should like to hear with which of our two friends you agree.

SOCRATES: What, Lysimachus, are you going to accept the opinion of the majority?

LYSIMACHUS: Why, yes, Socrates; what else am I to do?

SOCRATES: And would you do so too, Melesias? If you were deliberating about the gymnastic training of your son, would you follow the advice of the majority of us, or the opinion of the one who had been trained and exercised under a skilful master?

MELESIAS: The latter, Socrates; as would surely be reasonable.

SOCRATES: His one vote would be worth more than the vote of all us four?

MELESIAS: Certainly.

SOCRATES: And for this reason, as I imagine,--because a good decision is based on knowledge and not on numbers?

MELESIAS: To be sure.

SOCRATES: Must we not then first of all ask, whether 185a
there is any one of us who has knowledge of that about which
we are deliberating? If there is, let us take his advice, though
he be one only, and not mind the rest; if there is not, let us
seek further counsel. Is this a slight matter about which you
and Lysimachus are deliberating? Are you not risking the
greatest of your possessions? For children are your riches;
and upon their turning out well or ill depends the whole order of their father's house.

MELESIAS: That is true.

SOCRATES: Great care, then, is required in this matter?

MELESIAS: Certainly.

SOCRATES: Suppose, as I was just now saying, that we 185b
were considering, or wanting to consider, who was the best
trainer. Should we not select him who knew and had practised the art, and had the best teachers?

MELESIAS: I think that we should.

SOCRATES: But would there not arise a prior question
about the nature of the art of which we want to find the masters?

MELESIAS: I do not understand.

SOCRATES: Let me try to make my meaning plainer
then. I do not think that we have as yet decided what that
is about which we are consulting, when we ask which of us is
or is not skilled in the art, and has or has not had a teacher
of the art.

NICIAS: Why, Socrates, is not the question whether
young men ought or ought not to learn the art of fighting in
armour?

SOCRATES: Yes, Nicias; but there is also a prior question, which I may illustrate in this way: When a person considers about applying a medicine to the eyes, would you say

that he is consulting about the medicine or about the eyes?

NICIAS: About the eyes.

SOCRATES: And when he considers whether he shall set a bridle on a horse and at what time, he is thinking of the horse and not of the bridle?

NICIAS: True.

185e SOCRATES: And in a word, when he considers anything for the sake of another thing, he thinks of the end and not of the means?

NICIAS: Certainly.

SOCRATES: And when you call in an adviser, you should see whether he too is skilful in the accomplishment of the end which you have in view?

NICIAS: Most true.

SOCRATES: And at present we have in view some knowledge, of which the end is the soul of youth?

NICIAS: Yes.

SOCRATES: And we are enquiring, Which of us is skilful or successful in the treatment of the soul, and which of us has had good teachers?

LACHES: Well but, Socrates; did you never observe that some persons, who have had no teachers, are more skilful than those who have, in some things?

SOCRATES: Yes, Laches, I have observed that; but you would not be very willing to trust them if they only professed to be masters of their art, unless they could show some proof of their skill or excellence in one or more works.

LACHES: That is true.

SOCRATES: And therefore, Laches and Nicias, as Lysimachus and Melesias, in their anxiety to improve the minds of their sons, have asked our advice about them, we too should tell them who our teachers were, if we say that we have had any, and prove them to be in the first place men of merit and experienced trainers of the minds of youth and also to have been really our teachers. Or if any of us says that he has no teacher, but that he has works of his own to show; then he should point out to them what Athenians or strangers, bond or free, he is generally acknowledged to have improved. But if he can show neither teachers nor works, then he should tell them to look out for others; and not run the risk of spoiling the children of friends, and thereby incurring the most formidable accusation which can be brought against any one by those nearest to him. As for myself, Lysimachus and Melesias, I am the first to confess that I have never had a teacher of the art of virtue; although I have always from my earliest youth desired to have one. But I am too poor to give money to the Sophists, who are the only professors of moral improvement; and to this day I have never been able to discover the art myself, though I should not be surprised if Nicias or Laches may have discovered or learned it; for they are far wealthier than I am, and may therefore have learnt of others. And they are older too; so that they have had more time to make the discovery. And I really believe that they are able to educate a man; for unless they had been confident in their own knowledge, they would never have spoken thus decidedly of the pursuits which are advantageous or hurtful to a young man. I repose confidence in both of them; but I am surprised to find that they differ from one another. And therefore, Lysimachus, as Laches suggested that you should detain me, and not let me go until I answered, I in turn earnestly beseech and advise you to detain Laches and Nicias, and question them. I would have you say to them: Socrates avers that he has no knowledge of the matter--he is unable to decide which of you speaks truly; neither discoverer nor student is he of anything of the kind. But you, Laches and Nicias, should each of you tell us who is the most skilful educator whom you have ever known; and whether you invented the art yourselves, or learned of another; and if you learned, who were your respective teachers, and who were their brothers in the art; and then, if you are too much occupied in politics to teach us yourselves, let us go to them, and present them with gifts, or make interest with them, or both, in the hope that they may be induced to take charge of our children and of yours; and then they will not grow up inferior, and disgrace their ancestors. But if you are yourselves original discoverers in that field, give us some proof of your skill. Who are they who, having been inferior persons, have become under your care good and noble? For if this is your first attempt at education, there is a danger that you may be trying the experiment, not on the 'vile corpus' of a Carian slave, but on your own sons, or the sons of your friend, and, as the proverb says, 'break the large vessel in learning to make pots.' Tell us then, what qualities you claim or do not claim. Make them tell you that, Lysimachus, and do not let them off.

187C   LYSIMACHUS: I very much approve of the words of Socrates, my friends; but you, Nicias and Laches, must determine whether you will be questioned, and give an explanation about matters of this sort. Assuredly, I and Melesias would be greatly pleased to hear you answer the questions which Socrates asks, if you will: for I began by saying that we took you into our counsels because we thought that you would have attended to the subject, especially as you have children who, like our own, are nearly of an age to be educated. Well, then, if you have no objection, suppose that you take Socrates into partnership; and do you and he ask and answer one another's questions: for, as he has well said, we are deliberating about the most important of our concerns. I hope that you will see fit to comply with our request.

NICIAS: I see very clearly, Lysimachus, that you have only known Socrates' father, and have no acquaintance with Socrates himself: at least, you can only have known him when he was a child, and may have met him among his fellow-wardsmen, in company with his father, at a sacrifice, or at some other gathering. You clearly show that you have never known him since he arrived at manhood.

LYSIMACHUS: Why do you say that, Nicias?

NICIAS: Because you seem not to be aware that any one who has an intellectual affinity to Socrates and enters into conversation with him is liable to be drawn into an argument; and whatever subject he may start, he will be continually carried round and round by him, until at last he finds that he has to give an account both of his present and past life; and when he is once entangled, Socrates will not let him go until he has completely and thoroughly sifted him. Now I am used to his ways; and I know that he will certainly do as I say, and also that I myself shall be the sufferer; for I am fond of his conversation, Lysimachus. And I think that there is no harm in being reminded of any wrong thing which we are, or have been, doing: he who does not fly from reproof will be sure to take more heed of his after-life; as Solon says, he will wish and desire to be learning so long as he lives, and will not think that old age of itself brings wisdom. To me, to be cross-examined by Socrates is neither unusual nor unpleasant; indeed, I knew all along that where Socrates was, the argument would soon pass from our sons to ourselves; and therefore, I say that for my part, I am quite willing to discourse with Socrates in his own manner; but you had better ask our friend Laches what his feeling may be.

Laches = focused on the person

LACHES: I have but one feeling, Nicias, or (shall I say?) two feelings, about discussions. Some would think that I am a lover, and to others I may seem to be a hater of discourse; for when I hear a man discoursing of virtue, or of any sort of wisdom, who is a true man and worthy of his theme, I am delighted beyond measure: and I compare the man and his words, and note the harmony and correspondence of them. And such an one I deem to be the true musician, attuned to a fairer harmony than that of the lyre, or any pleasant instrument of music; for truly he has in his own life a harmony of words and deeds arranged, not in the Ionian, or in the Phrygian mode, nor yet in the Lydian, but in the true Hellenic mode, which is the Dorian, and no other. Such an one makes me merry with the sound of his voice; and when I hear him I am thought to be a lover of discourse; so eager am I in drinking in his words. But a man whose actions do not agree with his words is an annoyance to me; and the better he speaks

Laches admires Socrates

the more I hate him, and then I seem to be a hater of discourse. As to Socrates, I have no knowledge of his words, but of old, as would seem, I have had experience of his deeds; and his deeds show that free and noble sentiments are natural to him. And if his words accord, then I am of one mind with him, and shall be delighted to be interrogated by a man such as he is, and shall not be annoyed at having to learn of him: for I too agree with Solon, 'that I would fain grow old, learning many things.' But I must be allowed to add 'of the good only.' Socrates must be willing to allow that he is a good teacher, or I shall be a dull and uncongenial pupil: but that the teacher is younger, or not as yet in repute--anything of that sort is of no account with me. And therefore, Socrates, I give you notice that you may teach and confute me as much as ever you like, and also learn of me anything which I know. So high is the opinion which I have entertained of you ever since the day on which you were my companion in danger, and gave a proof of your valour such as only the man of merit can give. Therefore, say whatever you like, and do not mind about the difference of our ages.

189C SOCRATES: I cannot say that either of you show any reluctance to take counsel and advise with me.

LYSIMACHUS: But this is our proper business; and yours as well as ours, for I reckon you as one of us. Please then to take my place, and find out from Nicias and Laches what we want to know, for the sake of the youths, and talk and consult with them: for I am old, and my memory is bad; and I do not remember the questions which I am going to ask, or the answers to them; and if there is any interruption I am quite lost. I will therefore beg of you to carry on the proposed discussion by your selves; and I will listen, and Melesias and I will act upon your conclusions.

SOCRATES: Let us, Nicias and Laches, comply with the request of Lysimachus and Melesias. There will be no harm in asking ourselves the question which was first proposed to us: 'Who have been our own instructors in this sort of training, and whom have we made better?' But the other mode of carrying on the enquiry will bring us equally to the same

[margin notes] Bad for philosopher because needs to remember his argument

point, and will be more like proceeding from first principles. For if we knew that the addition of something would improve some other thing, and were able to make the addition, then, clearly, we must know how that about which we are advising may be best and most easily attained. Perhaps you do not understand what I mean. Then let me make my meaning plainer in this way. Suppose we knew that the addition of sight makes better the eyes which possess this gift, and also were able to impart sight to the eyes, then, clearly, we should know the nature of sight, and should be able to advise how this gift of sight may be best and most easily attained; but if we knew neither what sight is, nor what hearing is, we should not be very good medical advisers about the eyes or the ears, or about the best mode of giving sight and hearing to them.

LACHES: That is true, Socrates.   190b

SOCRATES: And are not our two friends, Laches, at this very moment inviting us to consider in what way the gift of virtue may be imparted to their sons for the improvement of their minds?

LACHES: Very true.

SOCRATES: Then must we not first know the nature of virtue? For how can we advise any one about the best mode of attaining something of which we are wholly ignorant?

LACHES: I do not think that we can, Socrates.

SOCRATES: Then, Laches, we may presume that we know the nature of virtue?

LACHES: Yes.

SOCRATES: And that which we know we must surely be able to tell?

LACHES: Certainly.

SOCRATES: I would not have us begin, my friend, with enquiring about the whole of virtue; for that may be more

than we can accomplish; let us first consider whether we
have a sufficient knowledge of a part; the enquiry will thus
probably be made easier to us.

LACHES: Let us do as you say, Socrates.

SOCRATES: Then which of the parts of virtue shall we
select? Must we not select that to which the art of fighting
in armour is supposed to conduce? And is not that generally
thought to be courage?

LACHES: Yes, certainly.

SOCRATES: Then, Laches, suppose that we first set
about determining the nature of courage, and in the second
place proceed to enquire how the young men may attain this
quality by the help of studies and pursuits. Tell me, if you
can, what is courage.

LACHES: Indeed, Socrates, I see no difficulty in answering; he is a man of courage who does not run away, but remains at his post and fights against the enemy; there can be
no mistake about that.

SOCRATES: Very good, Laches; and yet I fear that I did
not express myself clearly; and therefore you have answered
not the question which I intended to ask, but another.

LACHES: What do you mean, Socrates?

SOCRATES: I will endeavour to explain; you would call
a man courageous who remains at his post, and fights with
the enemy?

LACHES: Certainly I should.

SOCRATES: And so should I; but what would you say of
another man, who fights flying, instead of remaining?

LACHES: How flying?

SOCRATES: Why, as the Scythians are said to fight,
flying as well as pursuing; and as Homer says in praise of
the horses of Aeneas, that they knew 'how to pursue, and fly

quickly hither and thither'; and he passes an encomium on Aeneas himself, as having a knowledge of fear or flight, and calls him 'an author of fear or flight.'

LACHES: Yes, Socrates, and there Homer is right: for he was speaking of chariots, as you were speaking of the Scythian cavalry, who have that way of fighting; but the heavy-armed Greek fights, as I say, remaining in his rank.

SOCRATES: And yet, Laches, you must except the Lace-)9)c daemonians at Plataea, who, when they came upon the light shields of the Persians, are said not to have been willing to stand and fight, and to have fled; but when the ranks of the Persians were broken, they turned upon them like cavalry, and won the battle of Plataea.

LACHES: That is true. *Types of Courage*

SOCRATES: That was my meaning when I said that I was to blame in having put my question badly, and that this was the reason of your answering badly. For I meant to ask you not only about the courage of heavy-armed soldiers, but about the courage of cavalry and every other style of soldier; and not only who are courageous in war, but who are courageous in perils by sea, and who in disease, or in poverty, or again in politics, are courageous; and not only who are courageous against pain or fear, but mighty to contend against desires and pleasures, either fixed in their rank or turning upon their enemy. There is this sort of courage--is there not, Laches?

LACHES: Certainly, Socrates.

SOCRATES: And all these are courageous, but some have courage in pleasures, and some in pains: some in desires, and some in fears, and some are cowards under the same conditions, as I should imagine.

LACHES: Very true.

SOCRATES: Now I was asking about courage and cowardice in general. And I will begin with courage, and once more ask, What is that common quality, which is the same in all these cases, and which is called courage? Do you now understand what I mean?

LACHES: Not over well.

192a SOCRATES: I mean this: As I might ask what is that quality which is called quickness, and which is found in running, in playing the lyre, in speaking, in learning, and in many other similar actions, or rather which we possess in nearly every action that is worth mentioning of arms, legs, mouth, voice, mind;--would you not apply the term quickness to all of them?

LACHES: Quite true.

SOCRATES: And suppose I were to be asked by some one: What is that common quality, Socrates, which, in all these uses of the word, you call quickness? I should say the quality which accomplishes much in a little time--whether in running, speaking, or in any other sort of action.

LACHES: You would be quite correct.

SOCRATES: And now, Laches, do you try and tell me in like manner, What is that common quality which is called courage, and which includes all the various uses of the term when applied both to pleasure and pain, and in all the cases to which I was just now referring?

LACHES: I should say that courage is a sort of endurance of the soul, if I am to speak of the universal nature which pervades them all.

SOCRATES: But that is what we must do if we are to answer the question. And yet I cannot say that every kind of endurance is, in my opinion, to be deemed courage. Hear my reason: I am sure, Laches, that you would consider courage to be a very noble quality.

LACHES: Most noble, certainly.

SOCRATES: And you would say that a wise endurance is also good and noble?

LACHES: Very noble.

SOCRATES: But what would you say of a foolish endur- 192b
ance? Is not that, on the other hand, to be regarded as evil
and hurtful?

LACHES: True.

SOCRATES: And is anything noble which is evil and
hurtful?

LACHES: I ought not to say that, Socrates.

SOCRATES: Then you would not admit that sort of endurance to be courage-- for it is not noble, but courage is noble?

LACHES: You are right.

SOCRATES: Then, according to you, only the wise endurance is courage?

LACHES: True.

SOCRATES: But as to the epithet 'wise,'--wise in what? 192c
In all things small as well as great? For example, if a man
shows the quality of endurance in spending his money wisely, knowing that by spending he will acquire more in the end,
do you call him courageous?

LACHES: Assuredly not.

SOCRATES: Or, for example, if a man is a physician,
and his son, or some patient of his, has inflammation of the
lungs, and begs that he may be allowed to eat or drink something, and the other is firm and refuses; is that courage?

LACHES: No; that is not courage at all, any more than
the last.

SOCRATES: Again, take the case of one who endures in
war, and is willing to fight, and wisely calculates and knows
that others will help him, and that there will be fewer and
inferior men against him than there are with him; and suppose that he has also advantages of position; would you say

of such a one who endures with all this wisdom and prepa-
ration, that he, or some man in the opposing army who is
in the opposite circumstances to these and yet endures and
remains at his post, is the braver?

193b   LACHES: I should say that the latter, Socrates, was the
braver.

SOCRATES: But, surely, this is a foolish endurance in
comparison with the other?

LACHES: That is true.

SOCRATES: Then you would say that he who in an engagement of cavalry endures, having the knowledge of horse-
manship, is not so courageous as he who endures, having no
such knowledge?

LACHES: So I should say.

SOCRATES: And he who endures, having a knowledge
of the use of the sling, or the bow, or of any other art, is not
so courageous as he who endures, not having such a knowledge?

193c   LACHES: True.

SOCRATES: And he who descends into a well, and dives,
and holds out in this or any similar action, having no knowledge of diving, or the like, is, as you would say, more courageous than those who have this knowledge?

LACHES: Why, Socrates, what else can a man say?

SOCRATES: Nothing, if that be what he thinks.

LACHES: But that is what I do think.

SOCRATES: And yet men who thus run risks and endure are foolish, Laches, in comparison of those who do the
same things, having the skill to do them.

LACHES: That is true.

193d   SOCRATES: But foolish boldness and endurance appeared before to be base and hurtful to us.

LACHES: Quite true.

SOCRATES: Whereas courage was acknowledged to be a noble quality.

LACHES: True.

SOCRATES: And now on the contrary we are saying that the foolish endurance, which was before held in dishonour, is courage.

LACHES: Very true.

SOCRATES: And are we right in saying so?

LACHES: Indeed, Socrates, I am sure that we are not right.

SOCRATES: Then according to your statement, you and I, Laches, are not attuned to the Dorian mode, which is a harmony of words and deeds; for our deeds are not in accordance with our words. Any one would say that we had courage who saw us in action, but not, I imagine, he who heard us talking about courage just now.

LACHES: That is most true.

SOCRATES: And is this condition of ours satisfactory?

LACHES: Quite the reverse.

SOCRATES: Suppose, however, that we admit the principle of which we are speaking to a certain extent.

LACHES: To what extent and what principle do you mean?

SOCRATES: The principle of endurance. We too must endure and persevere in the enquiry, and then courage will not laugh at our faint-heartedness in searching for courage; which after all may, very likely, be endurance.

LACHES: I am ready to go on, Socrates; and yet I am

unused to investigations of this sort. But the spirit of contro-versy has been aroused in me by what has been said; and I am really grieved at being thus unable to express my mean-ing. For I fancy that I do know the nature of courage; but, somehow or other, she has slipped away from me, and I can-not get hold of her and tell her nature.

SOCRATES: But, my dear friend, should not the good sportsman follow the track, and not be lazy?

LACHES: Certainly, he should.

SOCRATES: And shall we invite Nicias to join us? he may be better at the sport than we are. What do you say?

LACHES: I should like that.

194c SOCRATES: Come then, Nicias, and do what you can to help your friends, who are tossing on the waves of argument, and at the last gasp: you see our extremity, and may save us and also settle your own opinion, if you will tell us what you think about courage.

NICIAS: I have been thinking, Socrates, that you and Laches are not defining courage in the right way; for you have forgotten an excellent saying which I have heard from your own lips.

SOCRATES: What is it, Nicias?

194d NICIAS: I have often heard you say that 'Every man is good in that in which he is wise, and bad in that in which he is unwise.'

SOCRATES: That is certainly true, Nicias.

NICIAS: And therefore if the brave man is good, he is also wise.

SOCRATES: Do you hear him, Laches?

LACHES: Yes, I hear him, but I do not very well under-stand him.

SOCRATES: I think that I understand him; and he appears to me to mean that courage is a sort of wisdom.

LACHES: What can he possibly mean, Socrates?

SOCRATES: That is a question which you must ask of
himself.   194e

LACHES: Yes.

SOCRATES: Tell him then, Nicias, what you mean by
this wisdom; for you surely do not mean the wisdom which
plays the flute?

NICIAS: Certainly not.

SOCRATES: Nor the wisdom which plays the lyre?

NICIAS: No.

SOCRATES: But what is this knowledge then, and of
what?

LACHES: I think that you put the question to him very
well, Socrates; and I would like him to say what is the nature
of this knowledge or wisdom.

NICIAS: I mean to say, Laches, that courage is the   195a
knowledge of that which inspires fear or confidence in war,
or in anything.

LACHES: How strangely he is talking, Socrates.

SOCRATES: Why do you say so, Laches?

LACHES: Why, surely courage is one thing, and wisdom
another.

SOCRATES: That is just what Nicias denies.

LACHES: Yes, that is what he denies; but he is so silly.

SOCRATES: Suppose that we instruct instead of abus-
ing him?

NICIAS: Laches does not want to instruct me, Socrates;
but having been proved to be talking nonsense himself, he

wants to prove that I have been doing the same.

LACHES: Very true, Nicias; and you are talking nonsense, as I shall endeavour to show. Let me ask you a question: Do not physicians know the dangers of disease? or do the courageous know them? or are the physicians the same as the courageous?

NICIAS: Not at all.

LACHES: No more than the husbandmen who know the dangers of husbandry, or than other craftsmen, who have a knowledge of that which inspires them with fear or confidence in their own arts, and yet they are not courageous a whit the more for that.

SOCRATES: What is Laches saying, Nicias? He appears to be saying something of importance.

NICIAS: Yes, he is saying something, but it is not true.

SOCRATES: How so?

NICIAS: Why, because he does not see that the physician's knowledge only extends to the nature of health and disease: he can tell the sick man no more than this. Do you imagine, Laches, that the physician knows whether health or disease is the more terrible to a man? Had not many a man better never get up from a sick bed? I should like to know whether you think that life is always better than death. May not death often be the better of the two?

LACHES: Yes certainly so in my opinion.

NICIAS: And do you think that the same things are terrible to those who had better die, and to those who had better live?

LACHES: Certainly not.

NICIAS: And do you suppose that the physician or any other artist knows this, or any one indeed, except he who is skilled in the grounds of fear and hope? And him I call the courageous.

SOCRATES: Do you understand his meaning, Laches?

LACHES: Yes; I suppose that, in his way of speaking, 195e
the soothsayers are courageous. For who but one of them
can know to whom to die or to live is better? And yet Nicias,
would you allow that you are yourself a soothsayer, or are
you neither a soothsayer nor courageous?

NICIAS: What! do you mean to say that the soothsayer
ought to know the grounds of hope or fear?

LACHES: Indeed I do: who but he?

NICIAS: Much rather I should say he of whom I speak;
for the soothsayer ought to know only the signs of things
that are about to come to pass, whether death or disease, or
loss of property, or victory, or defeat in war, or in any sort of
contest; but to whom the suffering or not suffering of these
things will be for the best, can no more be decided by the
soothsayer than by one who is no soothsayer.

LACHES: I cannot understand what Nicias would be at,
Socrates; for he represents the courageous man as neither a
soothsayer, nor a physician, nor in any other character, unless he means to say that he is a god. My opinion is that he
does not like honestly to confess that he is talking nonsense,
but that he shuffles up and down in order to conceal the difficulty into which he has got himself. You and I, Socrates,
might have practised a similar shuffle just now, if we had
only wanted to avoid the appearance of inconsistency. And if
we had been arguing in a court of law there might have been
reason in so doing; but why should a man deck himself out
with vain words at a meeting of friends such as this?

SOCRATES: I quite agree with you, Laches, that he 196c
should not. But perhaps Nicias is serious, and not merely
talking for the sake of talking. Let us ask him just to explain
what he means, and if he has reason on his side we will agree
with him; if not, we will instruct him.

LACHES: Do you, Socrates, if you like, ask him: I think
that I have asked enough.

SOCRATES: I do not see why I should not; and my question will do for both of us.

LACHES: Very good.

196d SOCRATES: Then tell me, Nicias, or rather tell us, for Laches and I are partners in the argument: Do you mean to affirm that courage is the knowledge of the grounds of hope and fear?

NICIAS: I do.

SOCRATES: And not every man has this knowledge; the physician and the soothsayer have it not; and they will not be courageous unless they acquire it--that is what you were saying?

NICIAS: I was.

SOCRATES: Then this is certainly not a thing which every pig would know, as the proverb says, and therefore he could not be courageous.

NICIAS: I think not.

196e SOCRATES: Clearly not, Nicias; not even such a big pig as the Crommyonian sow would be called by you courageous. And this I say not as a joke, but because I think that he who assents to your doctrine, that courage is the knowledge of the grounds of fear and hope, cannot allow that any wild beast is courageous, unless he admits that a lion, or a leopard, or perhaps a boar, or any other animal, has such a degree of wisdom that he knows things which but a few human beings ever know by reason of their difficulty. He who takes your view of courage must affirm that a lion, and a stag, and a bull, and a monkey, have equally little pretensions to courage.

197a LACHES: Capital, Socrates; by the gods, that is truly good. And I hope, Nicias, that you will tell us whether these animals, which we all admit to be courageous, are really wiser than mankind; or whether you will have the boldness, in the face of universal opinion, to deny their courage.

NICIAS: Why, Laches, I do not call animals or any other things which have no fear of dangers, because they are ignorant of them, courageous, but only fearless and senseless. Do you imagine that I should call little children courageous, which fear no dangers because they know none? There is a difference, to my way of thinking, between fearlessness and courage. I am of opinion that thoughtful courage is a quality possessed by very few, but that rashness and boldness, and fearlessness, which has no forethought, are very common qualities possessed by many men, many women, many children, many animals. And you, and men in general, call by the term 'courageous' actions which I call rash;--my courageous actions are wise actions.

LACHES: Behold, Socrates, how admirably, as he thinks, he dresses himself out in words, while seeking to deprive of the honour of courage those whom all the world acknowledges to be courageous.

NICIAS: Not so, Laches, but do not be alarmed; for I am quite willing to say of you and also of Lamachus, and of many other Athenians, that you are courageous and therefore wise.

LACHES: I could answer that; but I would not have you cast in my teeth that I am a haughty Aexonian.

SOCRATES: Do not answer him, Laches; I rather fancy 197d that you are not aware of the source from which his wisdom is derived. He has got all this from my friend Damon, and Damon is always with Prodicus, who, of all the Sophists, is considered to be the best puller to pieces of words of this sort.

LACHES: Yes, Socrates; and the examination of such niceties is a much more suitable employment for a Sophist than for a great statesman whom the city chooses to preside over her.

SOCRATES: Yes, my sweet friend, but a great states- 197e man is likely to have a great intelligence. And I think that the view which is implied in Nicias' definition of courage is worthy of examination.

LACHES: Then examine for yourself, Socrates.

SOCRATES: That is what I am going to do, my dear friend. Do not, however, suppose I shall let you out of the partnership; for I shall expect you to apply your mind, and join with me in the consideration of the question.

LACHES: I will if you think that I ought.

198a SOCRATES: Yes, I do; but I must beg of you, Nicias, to begin again. You remember that we originally considered courage to be a part of virtue.

NICIAS: Very true.

SOCRATES: And you yourself said that it was a part; and there were many other parts, all of which taken together are called virtue.

NICIAS: Certainly.

SOCRATES: Do you agree with me about the parts? For I say that justice, temperance, and the like, are all of them parts of virtue as well as courage. Would you not say the same?

198b NICIAS: Certainly.

SOCRATES: Well then, so far we are agreed. And now let us proceed a step, and try to arrive at a similar agreement about the fearful and the hopeful: I do not want you to be thinking one thing and myself another. Let me then tell you my own opinion, and if I am wrong you shall set me right: in my opinion the terrible and the hopeful are the things which do or do not create fear, and fear is not of the present, nor of the past, but is of future and expected evil. Do you not agree to that, Laches?

LACHES: Yes, Socrates, entirely.

198c SOCRATES: That is my view, Nicias; the terrible things, as I should say, are the evils which are future; and the hopeful are the good or not evil things which are future. Do you or do you not agree with me?

NICIAS: I agree.

SOCRATES: And the knowledge of these things you call courage?

NICIAS: Precisely.

SOCRATES: And now let me see whether you agree with Laches and myself as to a third point.

NICIAS: What is that?

SOCRATES: I will tell you. He and I have a notion that |98d| there is not one knowledge or science of the past, another of the present, a third of what is likely to be best and what will be best in the future; but that of all three there is one science only: for example, there is one science of medicine which is concerned with the inspection of health equally in all times, present, past, and future; and one science of husbandry in like manner, which is concerned with the productions of the earth in all times. As to the art of the general, you yourselves will be my witnesses that he has an excellent foreknowledge of the future, and that he claims to be the master and not the servant of the soothsayer, because he knows better what is happening or is likely to happen in war: and accordingly the law places the soothsayer under the general, and not the general under the soothsayer. Am I not correct in saying so, Laches?

LACHES: Quite correct.

SOCRATES: And do you, Nicias, also acknowledge that the same science has understanding of the same things, whether future, present, or past?

NICIAS: Yes, indeed Socrates; that is my opinion.

SOCRATES: And courage, my friend, is, as you say, a knowledge of the fearful and of the hopeful?   199b

NICIAS: Yes.

SOCRATES: And the fearful, and the hopeful, are admitted to be future goods and future evils?

NICIAS: True.

SOCRATES: And the same science has to do with the same things in the future or at any time?

NICIAS: That is true.

SOCRATES: Then courage is not the science which is concerned with the fearful and hopeful, for they are future only; courage, like the other sciences, is concerned not only with good and evil of the future, but of the present and past, and of any time?

NICIAS: That, as I suppose, is true.

SOCRATES: Then the answer which you have given, Nicias, includes only a third part of courage; but our question extended to the whole nature of courage: and according to your view, that is, according to your present view, courage is not only the knowledge of the hopeful and the fearful, but seems to include nearly every good and evil without reference to time. What do you say to that alteration in your statement?

NICIAS: I agree, Socrates.

SOCRATES: But then, my dear friend, if a man knew all good and evil, and how they are, and have been, and will be produced, would he not be perfect, and wanting in no virtue, whether justice, or temperance, or holiness? He would possess them all, and he would know which were dangers and which were not, and guard against them whether they were supernatural or natural; and he would provide the good, as he would know how to deal both with gods or men.

NICIAS: I think, Socrates, that there is a great deal of truth in what you say.

SOCRATES: But then, Nicias, courage, according to this new definition of yours, instead of being a part of virtue only, will be all virtue?

NICIAS: It would seem so.

SOCRATES: But we were saying that courage is one of the parts of virtue?

NICIAS: Yes, that was what we were saying.

SOCRATES: And that is in contradiction with our present view?

NICIAS: That appears to be the case.

SOCRATES: Then, Nicias, we have not discovered what courage is.

NICIAS: We have not.

LACHES: And yet, friend Nicias, I imagined that you 2009 would have made the discovery, when you were so contemptuous of the answers which I made to Socrates. I had very great hopes that you would have been enlightened by the wisdom of Damon.

NICIAS: I perceive, Laches, that you think nothing of having displayed your ignorance of the nature of courage, but you look only to see whether I have not made a similar display; and if we are both equally ignorant of the things which a man who is good for anything should know, that, I suppose, will be of no consequence. You certainly appear to me very like the rest of the world, looking at your neighbour and not at yourself. I am of opinion that enough has been said on the subject which we have been discussing; and if anything has been imperfectly said, that may be hereafter corrected by the help of Damon, whom you think to laugh down, although you have never seen him, and with the help of others. And when I am satisfied myself, I will freely impart my satisfaction to you, for I think that you are very much in want of knowledge.

LACHES: You are a philosopher, Nicias; of that I am aware: nevertheless I would recommend Lysimachus and

Melesias not to take you and me as advisers about the education of their children; but, as I said at first, they should ask Socrates and not let him off; if my own sons were old enough, I would have asked him myself.

200d NICIAS: To that I quite agree, if Socrates is willing to take them under his charge. I should not wish for any one else to be the tutor of Niceratus. But I observe that when I mention the matter to him he recommends to me some other tutor and refuses himself. Perhaps he may be more ready to listen to you, Lysimachus.

LYSIMACHUS: He ought, Nicias: for certainly I would do things for him which I would not do for many others. What do you say, Socrates--will you comply? And are you ready to give assistance in the improvement of the youths?

200e SOCRATES: Indeed, Lysimachus, I should be very wrong in refusing to aid in the improvement of anybody. And if I had shown in this conversation that I had a knowledge which Nicias and Laches have not, then I admit that you would be right in inviting me to perform this duty; but as we are all in the same perplexity, why should one of us be preferred to another? I certainly think that no one should; and under these circumstances, let me offer you a piece of advice (and this need not go further than ourselves). I maintain, my friends, 201a that every one of us should seek out the best teacher whom he can find, first for ourselves, who are greatly in need of one, and then for the youth, regardless of expense or anything. But I cannot advise that we remain as we are. And if any one laughs at us for going to school at our age, I would quote to them the authority of Homer, who says, that

'Modesty is not good for a needy man.'

Let us then, regardless of what may be said of us, make the education of the youths our own education.

201c LYSIMACHUS: I like your proposal, Socrates; and as I am the oldest, I am also the most eager to go to school with the boys. Let me beg a favour of you: Come to my house to-morrow at dawn, and we will advise about these matters.

they want socrates to teach their boys

For the present, let us make an end of the conversation.

SOCRATES: I will come to you to-morrow, Lysimachus, as you propose, <u>God willing.</u>

↳ maybe it is not worth his time

CHARMIDES

PREFACE TO THE FIRST EDITION.

The Text which has been mostly followed in this Translation of Plato is the latest 8vo. edition of Stallbaum; the principal deviations are noted at the bottom of the page.

I have to acknowledge many obligations to old friends and pupils. These are:--Mr. John Purves, Fellow of Balliol College, with whom I have revised about half of the entire Translation; the Rev. Professor Campbell, of St. Andrews, who has helped me in the revision of several parts of the work, especially of the Theaetetus, Sophist, and Politicus; Mr. Robinson Ellis, Fellow of Trinity College, and Mr. Alfred Robinson, Fellow of New College, who read with me the Cratylus and the Gorgias; Mr. Paravicini, Student of Christ Church, who assisted me in the Symposium; Mr. Raper, Fellow of Queen's College, Mr. Monro, Fellow of Oriel College, and Mr. Shadwell, Student of Christ Church, who gave me similar assistance in the Laws. Dr. Greenhill, of Hastings, has also kindly sent me remarks on the physiological part of the Timaeus, which I have inserted as corrections under the head of errata at the end of the Introduction. The degree of accuracy which I have been enabled to attain is in great measure due to these gentlemen, and I heartily thank them for the pains and time which they have bestowed on my work.

I have further to explain how far I have received help from other labourers in the same field. The books which I have found of most use are Steinhart and Muller's German Translation of Plato with Introductions; Zeller's 'Philosophie der Griechen,' and 'Platonische Studien;' Susemihl's 'Genetische Entwickelung der Paltonischen Philosophie;' Hermann's 'Geschichte der Platonischen Philosophie;' Bonitz, 'Platonische Studien;' Stallbaum's Notes and Introductions; Professor Campbell's editions of the 'Theaetetus,' the 'Sophist,' and the 'Politicus;' Professor Thompson's 'Phaedrus;' Th. Martin's 'Etudes sur le Timee;' Mr. Poste's edition and translation of the 'Philebus;' the Translation of the 'Republic,' by Messrs. Davies and Vaughan, and the Translation of the 'Gorgias,' by Mr. Cope.

I have also derived much assistance from the great work
of Mr. Grote, which contains excellent analyses of the Dialogues, and is rich in original thoughts and observations. I
agree with him in rejecting as futile the attempt of Schleiermacher and others to arrange the Dialogues of Plato into a
harmonious whole. Any such arrangement appears to me
not only to be unsupported by evidence, but to involve an
anachronism in the history of philosophy. There is a common spirit in the writings of Plato, but not a unity of design
in the whole, nor perhaps a perfect unity in any single Dialogue. The hypothesis of a general plan which is worked out
in the successive Dialogues is an after-thought of the critics
who have attributed a system to writings belonging to an age
when system had not as yet taken possession of philosophy.

If Mr. Grote should do me the honour to read any portion
of this work he will probably remark that I have endeav-
oured to approach Plato from a point of view which is opposed to his own. The aim of the Introductions in these vol-
umes has been to represent Plato as the father of Idealism,
who is not to be measured by the standard of utilitarianism
or any other modern philosophical system. He is the poet or
maker of ideas, satisfying the wants of his own age, provid-
ing the instruments of thought for future generations. He
is no dreamer, but a great philosophical genius struggling
with the unequal conditions of light and knowledge under
which he is living. He may be illustrated by the writings of
moderns, but he must be interpreted by his own, and by his
place in the history of philosophy. We are not concerned to
determine what is the residuum of truth which remains for
ourselves. His truth may not be our truth, and nevertheless
may have an extraordinary value and interest for us.

I cannot agree with Mr. Grote in admitting as genuine
all the writings commonly attributed to Plato in antiquity,
any more than with Schaarschmidt and some other German
critics who reject nearly half of them. The German critics,
to whom I refer, proceed chiefly on grounds of internal evidence; they appear to me to lay too much stress on the variety of doctrine and style, which must be equally acknowledged

as a fact, even in the Dialogues regarded by Schaarschmidt as genuine, e.g. in the Phaedrus, or Symposium, when compared with the Laws. He who admits works so different in style and matter to have been the composition of the same author, need have no difficulty in admitting the Sophist or the Politicus. (The negative argument adduced by the same school of critics, which is based on the silence of Aristotle, is not worthy of much consideration. For why should Aristotle, because he has quoted several Dialogues of Plato, have quoted them all? Something must be allowed to chance, and to the nature of the subjects treated of in them.) On the other hand, Mr. Grote trusts mainly to the Alexandrian Canon. But I hardly think that we are justified in attributing much weight to the authority of the Alexandrian librarians in an age when there was no regular publication of books, and every temptation to forge them; and in which the writings of a school were naturally attributed to the founder of the school. And even without intentional fraud, there was an inclination to believe rather than to enquire. Would Mr. Grote accept as genuine all the writings which he finds in the lists of learned ancients attributed to Hippocrates, to Xenophon, to Aristotle? The Alexandrian Canon of the Platonic writings is deprived of credit by the admission of the Epistles, which are not only unworthy of Plato, and in several passages plagiarized from him, but flagrantly at variance with historical fact. It will be seen also that I do not agree with Mr. Grote's views about the Sophists; nor with the low estimate which he has formed of Plato's Laws; nor with his opinion respecting Plato's doctrine of the rotation of the earth. But I 'am not going to lay hands on my father Parmenides' (Soph.), who will, I hope, forgive me for differing from him on these points. I cannot close this Preface without expressing my deep respect for his noble and gentle character, and the great services which he has rendered to Greek Literature.

Balliol College, January, 1871.

PREFACE TO THE SECOND AND THIRD EDITIONS.

In publishing a Second Edition (1875) of the Dialogues of Plato in English, I had to acknowledge the assistance of several friends: of the Rev. G.G. Bradley, Master of University College, now Dean of Westminster, who sent me some valuable remarks on the Phaedo; of Dr. Greenhill, who had again revised a portion of the Timaeus; of Mr. R.L. Nettleship, Fellow and Tutor of Balliol College, to whom I was indebted for an excellent criticism of the Parmenides; and, above all, of the Rev. Professor Campbell of St. Andrews, and Mr. Paravicini, late Student of Christ Church and Tutor of Balliol College, with whom I had read over the greater part of the translation. I was also indebted to Mr. Evelyn Abbott, Fellow and Tutor of Balliol College, for a complete and accurate index.

In this, the Third Edition, I am under very great obligations to Mr. Matthew Knight, who has not only favoured me with valuable suggestions throughout the work, but has largely extended the Index (from 61 to 175 pages) and translated the Eryxias and Second Alcibiades; and to Mr Frank Fletcher, of Balliol College, my Secretary. I am also considerably indebted to Mr. J.W. Mackail, late Fellow of Balliol College, who read over the Republic in the Second Edition and noted several inaccuracies.

In both editions the Introductions to the Dialogues have been enlarged, and essays on subjects having an affinity to the Platonic Dialogues have been introduced into several of them. The analyses have been corrected, and innumerable alterations have been made in the Text. There have been added also, in the Third Edition, headings to the pages and a marginal analysis to the text of each dialogue.

At the end of a long task, the translator may without impropriety point out the difficulties which he has had to encounter. These have been far greater than he would have anticipated; nor is he at all sanguine that he has succeeded in overcoming them. Experience has made him feel that a translation, like a picture, is dependent for its effect on very minute touches; and that it is a work of infinite pains, to be returned to in many moods and viewed in different lights.

I. An English translation ought to be idiomatic and interesting, not only to the scholar, but to the unlearned reader. Its object should not simply be to render the words of one language into the words of another or to preserve the construction and order of the original;--this is the ambition of a schoolboy, who wishes to show that he has made a good use of his Dictionary and Grammar; but is quite unworthy of the translator, who seeks to produce on his reader an impression similar or nearly similar to that produced by the original. To him the feeling should be more important than the exact word. He should remember Dryden's quaint admonition not to 'lacquey by the side of his author, but to mount up behind him.' (Dedication to the Aeneis.) He must carry in his mind a comprehensive view of the whole work, of what has preceded and of what is to follow,--as well as of the meaning of particular passages. His version should be based, in the first instance, on an intimate knowledge of the text; but the precise order and arrangement of the words may be left to fade out of sight, when the translation begins to take shape. He must form a general idea of the two languages, and reduce the one to the terms of the other. His work should be rhythmical and varied, the right admixture of words and syllables, and even of letters, should be carefully attended to; above all, it should be equable in style. There must also be quantity, which is necessary in prose as well as in verse: clauses, sentences, paragraphs, must be in due proportion. Metre and even rhyme may be rarely admitted; though neither is a legitimate element of prose writing, they may help to lighten a cumbrous expression (Symp.). The translation should retain as far as possible the characteristic qualities of the ancient writer--his freedom, grace, simplicity, stateliness, weight, precision; or the best part of him will be lost to the English reader. It should read as an original work, and should also be the most faithful transcript which can be made of the language from which the translation is taken, consistently with the first requirement of all, that it be English. Further, the translation being English, it should also be perfectly intelligible in itself without reference to the Greek, the English being really the more lucid and exact of the two languages. In some respects it may be maintained that ordinary English writing, such as the newspaper article, is superior to Plato: at any rate it is couched in language which is very rarely obscure. On the other hand, the greatest writers of Greece, Thucydides, Plato, Aeschylus, Sophocles, Pindar, Demosthenes, are generally those which are found to be most difficult and to diverge most widely from the English idiom. The translator will often have to convert the more abstract Greek into the more concrete English, or vice versa, and he ought not to force upon one language the character of another. In some cases, where the order is confused, the expression feeble, the emphasis misplaced, or the sense somewhat faulty, he will not strive in his rendering to reproduce these characteristics, but will re-write the passage as his author would have written it at first, had he not been 'nodding'; and he will not hesitate to supply anything which, owing to the genius of the language or some accident of composition, is omitted in the Greek, but is necessary to make the English clear and consecutive.

It is difficult to harmonize all these conflicting elements. In a translation of Plato what may be termed the interests of the Greek and English are often at war with one another. In framing the English sentence we are insensibly diverted from the exact meaning of the Greek; when we return to the Greek we are apt to cramp and overlay the English. We substitute, we compromise, we give and take, we add a little here and leave out a little there. The translator may sometimes be allowed to sacrifice minute accuracy for the sake of clearness and sense. But he is not therefore at liberty to omit words and turns of expression which the English language is quite capable of supplying. He must be patient and self-controlled; he must not be easily run away with. Let him never allow the attraction of a favourite expression, or a sonorous cadence, to overpower his better judgment, or think much of an ornament which is out of keeping with the general character of his work. He must ever be casting his eyes upwards from the copy to the original, and down again from the original to the copy (Rep.). His calling is not held in much honour by the world of scholars; yet he himself may be excused for thinking it a kind of glory to have lived so many years in the companionship of one of the greatest of human intelligences, and in some degree, more perhaps than others, to have had the privilege of understanding him (Sir Joshua Reynolds' Lectures: Disc. xv.).

There are fundamental differences in Greek and English, of which some may be managed while others remain intractable. (1). The structure of the Greek language is partly adversative and alternative, and partly inferential; that is to say, the members of a sentence are either opposed to one another, or one of them expresses the cause or effect or condition or reason of another. The two tendencies may be called the horizontal and perpendicular lines of the language; and the opposition or inference is often much more one of words than of ideas. But modern languages have rubbed off this adversative and inferential form: they have fewer links of connection, there is less mortar in the interstices, and they are content to place sentences side by side, leaving their relation to one another to be gathered from their position or from the context. The difficulty of preserving the effect of the Greek is increased by the want of adversative and inferential particles in English, and by the nice sense of tautology which characterizes all modern languages. We cannot have two 'buts' or two 'fors' in the same sentence where the Greek repeats (Greek). There is a similar want of particles expressing the various gradations of objective and subjective thought-- (Greek) and the like, which are so thickly scattered over the Greek page. Further, we can only realize to a very imperfect degree the common distinction between (Greek), and the combination of the two suggests a subtle shade of negation which cannot be expressed in English. And while English is more dependent than Greek upon the apposition of clauses and sentences, yet there is a difficulty in using this form of construction owing to the want of case endings. For the same reason there cannot be an equal variety in the order of words or an equal nicety of emphasis in English as in Greek.

(2) The formation of the sentence and of the paragraph greatly differs in Greek and English. The lines by which they are divided are generally much more marked in modern languages than in ancient. Both sentences and paragraphs are more precise and definite--they do not run into one another. They are also more regularly developed from within. The sentence marks another step in an argument or a narrative or a statement; in reading a paragraph we silently turn over the page and arrive at some new view or aspect of the subject. Whereas in Plato we are not always certain where a sentence begins and ends; and paragraphs are few and far between. The language is distributed in a different way, and less articulated than in English. For it was long before the true use of the period was attained by the classical writers both in poetry or prose; it was (Greek). The balance of sentences and the introduction of paragraphs at suitable intervals must not be neglected if the harmony of the English language is to be preserved. And still a caution has to be added on the other side, that we must avoid giving it a numerical or mechanical character.

(3) This, however, is not one of the greatest difficulties of the translator; much greater is that which arises from the restriction of the use of the genders. Men and women in English are masculine and feminine, and there is a similar distinction of sex in the words denoting animals; but all things else, whether outward objects or abstract ideas, are relegated to the class of neuters. Hardly in some flight of poetry do we ever endue any of them with the characteristics of a sentient being, and then only by speaking of them in the feminine gender. The virtues may be pictured in female forms, but they are not so described in language; a ship is humorously supposed to be the sailor's bride; more doubtful are the personifications of church and country as females. Now the genius of the Greek language is the opposite of this. The same tendency to personification which is seen in the Greek mythology is common also in the language; and genders are attributed to things as well as persons according to their various degrees of strength and weakness; or from fanciful resemblances to the male or female form, or some analogy

too subtle to be discovered. When the gender of any object was once fixed, a similar gender was naturally assigned to similar objects, or to words of similar formation. This use of genders in the denotation of objects or ideas not only affects the words to which genders are attributed, but the words with which they are construed or connected, and passes into the general character of the style. Hence arises a difficulty in translating Greek into English which cannot altogether be overcome. Shall we speak of the soul and its qualities, of virtue, power, wisdom, and the like, as feminine or neuter? The usage of the English language does not admit of the former, and yet the life and beauty of the style are impaired by the latter. Often the translator will have recourse to the repetition of the word, or to the ambiguous 'they,' 'their,' etc.; for fear of spoiling the effect of the sentence by introducing 'it.' Collective nouns in Greek and English create a similar but lesser awkwardness.

(4) To use of relation is far more extended in Greek than in English. Partly the greater variety of genders and cases makes the connexion of relative and antecedent less ambiguous: partly also the greater number of demonstrative and relative pronouns, and the use of the article, make the correlation of ideas simpler and more natural. The Greek appears to have had an ear or intelligence for a long and complicated sentence which is rarely to be found in modern nations; and in order to bring the Greek down to the level of the modern, we must break up the long sentence into two or more short ones. Neither is the same precision required in Greek as in Latin or English, nor in earlier Greek as in later; there was nothing shocking to the contemporary of Thucydides and Plato in anacolutha and repetitions. In such cases the genius of the English language requires that the translation should be more intelligible than the Greek. The want of more distinctions between the demonstrative pronouns is also greatly felt. Two genitives dependent on one another, unless familiarised by idiom, have an awkward effect in English. Frequently the noun has to take the place of the pronoun. 'This' and 'that' are found repeating themselves to weariness in the rough draft of a translation. As in the previous case, while

the feeling of the modern language is more opposed to tautology, there is also a greater difficulty in avoiding it.

(5) Though no precise rule can be laid down about the repetition of words, there seems to be a kind of impertinence in presenting to the reader the same thought in the same words, repeated twice over in the same passage without any new aspect or modification of it. And the evasion of tautology--that is, the substitution of one word of precisely the same meaning for another--is resented by us equally with the repetition of words. Yet on the other hand the least difference of meaning or the least change of form from a substantive to an adjective, or from a participle to a verb, will often remedy the unpleasant effect. Rarely and only for the sake of emphasis or clearness can we allow an important word to be used twice over in two successive sentences or even in the same paragraph. The particles and pronouns, as they are of most frequent occurrence, are also the most troublesome. Strictly speaking, except a few of the commonest of them, 'and,' 'the,' etc., they ought not to occur twice in the same sentence. But the Greek has no such precise rules; and hence any literal translation of a Greek author is full of tautology. The tendency of modern languages is to become more correct as well as more perspicuous than ancient. And, therefore, while the English translator is limited in the power of expressing relation or connexion, by the law of his own language increased precision and also increased clearness are required of him. The familiar use of logic, and the progress of science, have in these two respects raised the standard. But modern languages, while they have become more exacting in their demands, are in many ways not so well furnished with powers of expression as the ancient classical ones.

Such are a few of the difficulties which have to be overcome in the work of translation; and we are far from having exhausted the list. (6) The excellence of a translation will consist, not merely in the faithful rendering of words, or in the composition of a sentence only, or yet of a single paragraph, but in the colour and style of the whole work. Equability of tone is best attained by the exclusive use of familiar and idiomatic words. But great care must be taken; for an idiomatic phrase, if an exception to the general style, is of itself a disturbing element. No word, however expressive and exact, should be employed, which makes the reader stop to think, or unduly attracts attention by difficulty and peculiarity, or disturbs the effect of the surrounding language. In general the style of one author is not appropriate to another; as in society, so in letters, we expect every man to have 'a good coat of his own,' and not to dress himself out in the rags of another. (a) Archaic expressions are therefore to be avoided. Equivalents may be occasionally drawn from Shakspere, who is the common property of us all; but they must be used sparingly. For, like some other men of genius of the Elizabethan and Jacobean age, he outdid the capabilities of the language, and many of the expressions which he introduced have been laid aside and have dropped out of use. (b) A similar principle should be observed in the employment of Scripture. Having a greater force and beauty than other language, and a religious association, it disturbs the even flow of the style. It may be used to reproduce in the translation the quaint effect of some antique phrase in the original, but rarely; and when adopted, it should have a certain freshness and a suitable 'entourage.' It is strange to observe that the most effective use of Scripture phraseology arises out of the application of it in a sense not intended by the author. (c) Another caution: metaphors differ in different languages, and the translator will often be compelled to substitute one for another, or to paraphrase them, not giving word for word, but diffusing over several words the more concentrated thought of the original. The Greek of Plato often goes beyond the English in its imagery: compare Laws, (Greek); Rep.; etc. Or again the modern word, which in substance is the nearest equivalent to the Greek, may be found to include associations alien to Greek life: e.g. (Greek), 'jurymen,' (Greek), 'the bourgeoisie.' (d) The translator has also to provide expressions for philosophical terms of very indefinite meaning in the more definite language of modern philosophy. And he must not allow discordant elements to enter into the work. For example, in translating Plato, it would equally be an anachronism to intrude on him the feeling and spirit of the Jewish or Christian Scriptures or the technical terms of the Hegelian or Darwinian philosophy.

(7) As no two words are precise equivalents (just as no two leaves of the forest are exactly similar), it is a mistaken attempt at precision always to translate the same Greek word by the same English word. There is no reason why in the New Testament (Greek) should always be rendered 'righteousness,' or (Greek) 'covenant.' In such cases the translator may be allowed to employ two words--sometimes when the two meanings occur in the same passage, varying them by an 'or'--e.g. (Greek), 'science' or 'knowledge,' (Greek), 'idea' or 'class,' (Greek), 'temperance' or 'prudence,'--at the point where the change of meaning occurs. If translations are intended not for the Greek scholar but for the general reader, their worst fault will be that they sacrifice the general effect and meaning to the over-precise rendering of words and forms of speech.

(8) There is no kind of literature in English which corresponds to the Greek Dialogue; nor is the English language easily adapted to it. The rapidity and abruptness of question and answer, the constant repetition of (Greek), etc., which Cicero avoided in Latin (de Amicit), the frequent occurrence of expletives, would, if reproduced in a translation, give offence to the reader. Greek has a freer and more frequent use of the Interrogative, and is of a more passionate and emotional character, and therefore lends itself with greater readiness to the dialogue form. Most of the so-called English Dialogues are but poor imitations of Plato, which fall very far short of the original. The breath of conversation, the subtle adjustment of question and answer, the lively play of fancy, the power of drawing characters, are wanting in them. But the Platonic dialogue is a drama as well as a dialogue, of which Socrates is the central figure, and there are lesser performers as well:--the insolence of Thrasymachus, the anger of Callicles and Anytus, the patronizing style of Protagoras, the self-consciousness of Prodicus and Hippias, are all part of the entertainment. To reproduce this living image the same

sort of effort is required as in translating poetry. The language, too, is of a finer quality; the mere prose English is slow in lending itself to the form of question and answer, and so the ease of conversation is lost, and at the same time the dialectical precision with which the steps of the argument are drawn out is apt to be impaired.

II. In the Introductions to the Dialogues there have been added some essays on modern philosophy, and on political and social life. The chief subjects discussed in these are Utility, Communism, the Kantian and Hegelian philosophies, Psychology, and the Origin of Language. (There have been added also in the Third Edition remarks on other subjects. A list of the most important of these additions is given at the end of this Preface.)

Ancient and modern philosophy throw a light upon one another: but they should be compared, not confounded. Although the connexion between them is sometimes accidental, it is often real. The same questions are discussed by them under different conditions of language and civilization; but in some cases a mere word has survived, while nothing or hardly anything of the pre-Socratic, Platonic, or Aristotelian meaning is retained. There are other questions familiar to the moderns, which have no place in ancient philosophy. The world has grown older in two thousand years, and has enlarged its stock of ideas and methods of reasoning. Yet the germ of modern thought is found in ancient, and we may claim to have inherited, notwithstanding many accidents of time and place, the spirit of Greek philosophy. There is, however, no continuous growth of the one into the other, but a new beginning, partly artificial, partly arising out of the questionings of the mind itself, and also receiving a stimulus from the study of ancient writings.

Considering the great and fundamental differences which exist in ancient and modern philosophy, it seems best that we should at first study them separately, and seek for the interpretation of either, especially of the ancient, from itself only, comparing the same author with himself and with his contemporaries, and with the general state of thought and feeling prevalent in his age. Afterwards comes the remoter light which they cast on one another. We begin to feel that the ancients had the same thoughts as ourselves, the same difficulties which characterize all periods of transition, almost the same opposition between science and religion. Although we cannot maintain that ancient and modern philosophy are one and continuous (as has been affirmed with more truth respecting ancient and modern history), for they are separated by an interval of a thousand years, yet they seem to recur in a sort of cycle, and we are surprised to find that the new is ever old, and that the teaching of the past has still a meaning for us.

III. In the preface to the first edition I expressed a strong opinion at variance with Mr. Grote's, that the so-called Epistles of Plato were spurious. His friend and editor, Professor Bain, thinks that I ought to give the reasons why I differ from so eminent an authority. Reserving the fuller discussion of the question for another place, I will shortly defend my opinion by the following arguments:--

(a) Because almost all epistles purporting to be of the classical age of Greek literature are forgeries. (Compare Bentley's Works (Dyce's Edition).) Of all documents this class are the least likely to be preserved and the most likely to be invented. The ancient world swarmed with them; the great libraries stimulated the demand for them; and at a time when there was no regular publication of books, they easily crept into the world.

(b) When one epistle out of a number is spurious, the remainder of the series cannot be admitted to be genuine, unless there be some independent ground for thinking them so: when all but one are spurious, overwhelming evidence is required of the genuineness of the one: when they are all similar in style or motive, like witnesses who agree in the same tale, they stand or fall together. But no one, not even Mr. Grote, would maintain that all the Epistles of Plato are genuine, and very few critics think that more than one of them is so. And they are clearly all written from the same motive, whether serious or only literary. Nor is there an example in Greek antiquity of a series of Epistles, continuous and yet coinciding with a succession of events extending over a great number of years.

The external probability therefore against them is enormous, and the internal probability is not less: for they are trivial and unmeaning, devoid of delicacy and subtlety, wanting in a single fine expression. And even if this be matter of dispute, there can be no dispute that there are found in them many plagiarisms, inappropriately borrowed, which is a common note of forgery. They imitate Plato, who never imitates either himself or any one else; reminiscences of the Republic and the Laws are continually recurring in them; they are too like him and also too unlike him, to be genuine (see especially Karsten, Commentio Critica de Platonis quae feruntur Epistolis). They are full of egotism, self-assertion, affectation, faults which of all writers Plato was most careful to avoid, and into which he was least likely to fall. They abound in obscurities, irrelevancies, solecisms, pleonasms, inconsistencies, awkwardnesses of construction, wrong uses of words. They also contain historical blunders, such as the statement respecting Hipparinus and Nysaeus, the nephews of Dion, who are said to 'have been well inclined to philosophy, and well able to dispose the mind of their brother Dionysius in the same course,' at a time when they could not have been more than six or seven years of age--also foolish allusions, such as the comparison of the Athenian empire to the empire of Darius, which show a spirit very different from that of Plato; and mistakes of fact, as e.g. about the Thirty Tyrants, whom the writer of the letters seems to have confused with certain inferior magistrates, making them in all fifty-one. These palpable errors and absurdities are absolutely irreconcilable with their genuineness. And as they appear to have a common parentage, the more they are studied, the more they will be found to furnish evidence against themselves. The Seventh, which is thought to be the most important of these Epistles, has affinities with the Third and the Eighth, and is quite as impossible and inconsistent as the rest. It is therefore involved in the same condemnation.--The final conclusion is that neither the Seventh nor any other of

them, when carefully analyzed, can be imagined to have pro-
ceeded from the hand or mind of Plato. The other testimonies
to the voyages of Plato to Sicily and the court of Dionysius
are all of them later by several centuries than the events to
which they refer. No extant writer mentions them older than
Cicero and Cornelius Nepos. It does not seem impossible that
so attractive a theme as the meeting of a philosopher and a
tyrant, once imagined by the genius of a Sophist, may have
passed into a romance which became famous in Hellas and
the world. It may have created one of the mists of history,
like the Trojan war or the legend of Arthur, which we are
unable to penetrate. In the age of Cicero, and still more in
that of Diogenes Laertius and Appuleius, many other leg-
ends had gathered around the personality of Plato,--more
voyages, more journeys to visit tyrants and Pythagorean
philosophers. But if, as we agree with Karsten in supposing,
they are the forgery of some rhetorician or sophist, we cannot agree with him in also supposing that they are of any
historical value, the rather as there is no early independent
testimony by which they are supported or with which they
can be compared.

IV. There is another subject to which I must briefly call
attention, lest I should seem to have overlooked it. Dr. Henry
Jackson, of Trinity College, Cambridge, in a series of articles
which he has contributed to the Journal of Philology, has put
forward an entirely new explanation of the Platonic 'Ideas.'
He supposes that in the mind of Plato they took, at different
times in his life, two essentially different forms:--an earlier
one which is found chiefly in the Republic and the Phaedo,
and a later, which appears in the Theaetetus, Philebus, Sophist, Politicus, Parmenides, Timaeus. In the first stage of his
philosophy Plato attributed Ideas to all things, at any rate
to all things which have classes or common notions: these
he supposed to exist only by participation in them. In the
later Dialogues he no longer included in them manufactured
articles and ideas of relation, but restricted them to 'types of
nature,' and having become convinced that the many cannot
be parts of the one, for the idea of participation in them he
substituted imitation of them. To quote Dr. Jackson's own

expressions,--'whereas in the period of the Republic and the Phaedo, it was proposed to pass through ontology to the sciences, in the period of the Parmenides and the Philebus, it is proposed to pass through the sciences to ontology': or, as he repeats in nearly the same words,--'whereas in the Republic and in the Phaedo he had dreamt of passing through ontology to the sciences, he is now content to pass through the sciences to ontology.'

This theory is supposed to be based on Aristotle's Metaphysics, a passage containing an account of the ideas, which hitherto scholars have found impossible to reconcile with the statements of Plato himself. The preparations for the new departure are discovered in the Parmenides and in the Theaetetus; and it is said to be expressed under a different form by the (Greek) and the (Greek) of the Philebus. The (Greek) of the Philebus is the principle which gives form and measure to the (Greek); and in the 'Later Theory' is held to be the (Greek) or (Greek) which converts the Infinite or Indefinite into ideas. They are neither (Greek) nor (Greek), but belong to the (Greek) which partakes of both.

With great respect for the learning and ability of Dr. Jackson, I find myself unable to agree in this newly fashioned doctrine of the Ideas, which he ascribes to Plato. I have not the space to go into the question fully; but I will briefly state some objections which are, I think, fatal to it.

(1) First, the foundation of his argument is laid in the Metaphysics of Aristotle. But we cannot argue, either from the Metaphysics, or from any other of the philosophical treatises of Aristotle, to the dialogues of Plato until we have ascertained the relation in which his so-called works stand to the philosopher himself. There is of course no doubt of the great influence exercised upon Greece and upon the world by Aristotle and his philosophy. But on the other hand almost every one who is capable of understanding the subject acknowledges that his writings have not come down to us in an authentic form like most of the dialogues of Plato. How much of them is to be ascribed to Aristotle's own hand, how much is due to his successors in the Peripatetic School, is a question

which has never been determined, and probably never can be, because the solution of it depends upon internal evidence only. To 'the height of this great argument' I do not propose to ascend. But one little fact, not irrelevant to the present discussion, will show how hopeless is the attempt to explain Plato out of the writings of Aristotle. In the chapter of the Metaphysics quoted by Dr. Jackson, about two octavo pages in length, there occur no less than seven or eight references to Plato, although nothing really corresponding to them can be found in his extant writings:--a small matter truly; but what a light does it throw on the character of the entire book in which they occur! We can hardly escape from the conclusion that they are not statements of Aristotle respecting Plato, but of a later generation of Aristotelians respecting a later generation of Platonists. (Compare the striking remark of the great Scaliger respecting the Magna Moralia:--Haec non sunt Aristotelis, tamen utitur auctor Aristotelis nomine tanquam suo.)

(2) There is no hint in Plato's own writings that he was conscious of having made any change in the Doctrine of Ideas such as Dr. Jackson attributes to him, although in the Republic the platonic Socrates speaks of 'a longer and a shorter way', and of a way in which his disciple Glaucon 'will be unable to follow him'; also of a way of Ideas, to which he still holds fast, although it has often deserted him (Philebus, Phaedo), and although in the later dialogues and in the Laws the reference to Ideas disappears, and Mind claims her own (Phil.; Laws). No hint is given of what Plato meant by the 'longer way' (Rep.), or 'the way in which Glaucon was unable to follow'; or of the relation of Mind to the Ideas. It might be said with truth that the conception of the Idea predominates in the first half of the Dialogues, which, according to the order adopted in this work, ends with the Republic, the 'conception of Mind' and a way of speaking more in agreement with modern terminology, in the latter half. But there is no reason to suppose that Plato's theory, or, rather, his various theories, of the Ideas underwent any definite change during his period of authorship. They are substantially the same in the twelfth Book of the Laws as in the Meno and

Phaedo; and since the Laws were written in the last decade of his life, there is no time to which this change of opinions can be ascribed. It is true that the theory of Ideas takes several different forms, not merely an earlier and a later one, in the various Dialogues. They are personal and impersonal, ideals and ideas, existing by participation or by imitation, one and many, in different parts of his writings or even in the same passage. They are the universal definitions of Socrates, and at the same time 'of more than mortal knowledge' (Rep.). But they are always the negations of sense, of matter, of generation, of the particular: they are always the subjects of knowledge and not of opinion; and they tend, not to diversity, but to unity. Other entities or intelligences are akin to them, but not the same with them, such as mind, measure, limit, eternity, essence (Philebus; Timaeus): these and similar terms appear to express the same truths from a different point of view, and to belong to the same sphere with them. But we are not justified, therefore, in attempting to identify them, any more than in wholly opposing them. The great oppositions of the sensible and intellectual, the unchangeable and the transient, in whatever form of words expressed, are always maintained in Plato. But the lesser logical distinctions, as we should call them, whether of ontology or predication, which troubled the pre-Socratic philosophy and came to the front in Aristotle, are variously discussed and explained. Thus far we admit inconsistency in Plato, but no further. He lived in an age before logic and system had wholly permeated language, and therefore we must not always expect to find in him systematic arrangement or logical precision:--'poema magis putandum.' But he is always true to his own context, the careful study of which is of more value to the interpreter than all the commentators and scholiasts put together.

(3) The conclusions at which Dr. Jackson has arrived are such as might be expected to follow from his method of procedure. For he takes words without regard to their connection, and pieces together different parts of dialogues in a purely arbitrary manner, although there is no indication that the author intended the two passages to be so combined, or that when he appears to be experimenting on the different points

of view from which a subject of philosophy may be regarded,
he is secretly elaborating a system. By such a use of language any premises may be made to lead to any conclusion.
I am not one of those who believe Plato to have been a mys-
tic or to have had hidden meanings; nor do I agree with Dr.
Jackson in thinking that 'when he is precise and dogmatic,
he generally contrives to introduce an element of obscurity
into the expostion' (J. of Philol.). The great master of language wrote as clearly as he could in an age when the minds
of men were clouded by controversy, and philosophical terms
had not yet acquired a fixed meaning. I have just said that
Plato is to be interpreted by his context; and I do not deny
that in some passages, especially in the Republic and Laws,
the context is at a greater distance than would be allowable
in a modern writer. But we are not therefore justified in con-
necting passages from different parts of his writings, or even
from the same work, which he has not himself joined. We
cannot argue from the Parmenides to the Philebus, or from
either to the Sophist, or assume that the Parmenides, the
Philebus, and the Timaeus were 'written simultaneously,'
or 'were intended to be studied in the order in which they
are here named (J. of Philol.) We have no right to connect
statements which are only accidentally similar. Nor is it safe
for the author of a theory about ancient philosophy to argue
from what will happen if his statements are rejected. For
those consequences may never have entered into the mind
of the ancient writer himself; and they are very likely to be
modern consequences which would not have been understood
by him. 'I cannot think,' says Dr. Jackson, 'that Plato would
have changed his opinions, but have nowhere explained the
nature of the change.' But is it not much more improbable
that he should have changed his opinions, and not stated in
an unmistakable manner that the most essential principle of
his philosophy had been reversed? It is true that a few of the
dialogues, such as the Republic and the Timaeus, or the Theaetetus and the Sophist, or the Meno and the Apology, contain
allusions to one another. But these allusions are superficial
and, except in the case of the Republic and the Laws, have no
philosophical importance. They do not affect the substance of

the work. It may be remarked further that several of the dialogues, such as the Phaedrus, the Sophist, and the Parmenides, have more than one subject. But it does not therefore follow that Plato intended one dialogue to succeed another, or that he begins anew in one dialogue a subject which he has left unfinished in another, or that even in the same dialogue he always intended the two parts to be connected with each other. We cannot argue from a casual statement found in the Parmenides to other statements which occur in the Philebus. Much more truly is his own manner described by himself when he says that 'words are more plastic than wax' (Rep.), and 'whither the wind blows, the argument follows'. The dialogues of Plato are like poems, isolated and separate works, except where they are indicated by the author himself to have an intentional sequence.

It is this method of taking passages out of their context and placing them in a new connexion when they seem to confirm a preconceived theory, which is the defect of Dr. Jackson's procedure. It may be compared, though not wholly the same with it, to that method which the Fathers practised, sometimes called 'the mystical interpretation of Scripture,' in which isolated words are separated from their context, and receive any sense which the fancy of the interpreter may suggest. It is akin to the method employed by Schleiermacher of arranging the dialogues of Plato in chronological order according to what he deems the true arrangement of the ideas contained in them. (Dr. Jackson is also inclined, having constructed a theory, to make the chronology of Plato's writings dependent upon it (See J. of Philol. and elsewhere.) It may likewise be illustrated by the ingenuity of those who employ symbols to find in Shakespeare a hidden meaning. In the three cases the error is nearly the same:--words are taken out of their natural context, and thus become destitute of any real meaning.

(4) According to Dr. Jackson's 'Later Theory,' Plato's Ideas, which were once regarded as the summa genera of all things, are now to be explained as Forms or Types of some things only,--that is to say, of natural objects: these we con-

ceive imperfectly, but are always seeking in vain to have a more perfect notion of them. He says (J. of Philol.) that 'Plato hoped by the study of a series of hypothetical or provisional classifications to arrive at one in which nature's distribution of kinds is approximately represented, and so to attain approximately to the knowledge of the ideas. But whereas in the Republic, and even in the Phaedo, though less hopefully, he had sought to convert his provisional definitions into final ones by tracing their connexion with the summum genus, the (Greek), in the Parmenides his aspirations are less ambitious,' and so on. But where does Dr. Jackson find any such notion as this in Plato or anywhere in ancient philosophy? Is it not an anachronism, gracious to the modern physical philosopher, and the more acceptable because it seems to form a link between ancient and modern philosophy, and between physical and metaphysical science; but really unmeaning?

(5) To this 'Later Theory' of Plato's Ideas I oppose the authority of Professor Zeller, who affirms that none of the passages to which Dr. Jackson appeals (Theaet.; Phil.; Tim.; Parm.) 'in the smallest degree prove his point'; and that in the second class of dialogues, in which the 'Later Theory of Ideas' is supposed to be found, quite as clearly as in the first, are admitted Ideas, not only of natural objects, but of properties, relations, works of art, negative notions (Theaet.; Parm.; Soph.); and that what Dr. Jackson distinguishes as the first class of dialogues from the second equally assert or imply that the relation of things to the Ideas, is one of participation in them as well as of imitation of them (Prof. Zeller's summary of his own review of Dr. Jackson, Archiv fur Geschichte der Philosophie.)

In conclusion I may remark that in Plato's writings there is both unity, and also growth and development; but that we must not intrude upon him either a system or a technical language.

Balliol College, October, 1891.

NOTE:

The chief additions to the Introductions in the Third Edition consist of Essays on the following subjects:--

1. Language.

2. The decline of Greek Literature.

3. The 'Ideas' of Plato and Modern Philosophy.

4. The myths of Plato.

5. The relation of the Republic, Statesman and Laws.

6. The legend of Atlantis.

7. Psychology.

8. Comparison of the Laws of Plato with Spartan and Athenian Laws and Institutions.

CHARMIDES.

INTRODUCTION.

The subject of the Charmides is Temperance or (Greek), a peculiarly Greek notion, which may also be rendered Moderation (Compare Cic. Tusc. '(Greek), quam soleo equidem tum temperantiam, tum moderationem appellare, nonnunquam etiam modestiam.'), Modesty, Discretion, Wisdom, without completely exhausting by all these terms the various associations of the word. It may be described as 'mens sana in corpore sano,' the harmony or due proportion of the higher and lower elements of human nature which 'makes a man his own master,' according to the definition of the Republic. In the accompanying translation the word has been rendered in different places either Temperance or Wisdom, as the connection seemed to require: for in the philosophy of Plato (Greek) still retains an intellectual element (as Socrates is also said to have identified (Greek) with (Greek): Xen. Mem.) and is not yet relegated to the sphere of moral virtue, as in the Nicomachean Ethics of Aristotle.

The beautiful youth, Charmides, who is also the most temperate of human beings, is asked by Socrates, 'What is Temperance?' He answers characteristically, (1) 'Quietness.' 'But Temperance is a fine and noble thing; and quietness in many or most cases is not so fine a thing as quickness.' He tries again and says (2) that temperance is modesty. But this again is set aside by a sophistical application of Homer: for temperance is good as well as noble, and Homer has declared that 'modesty is not good for a needy man.' (3) Once more Charmides makes the attempt. This time he gives a definition which he has heard, and of which Socrates conjectures that Critias must be the author: 'Temperance is doing one's own business.' But the artisan who makes another man's shoes may be temperate, and yet he is not doing his own business; and temperance defined thus would be opposed to the division of labour which exists in every temperate or well-ordered state. How is this riddle to be explained?

Critias, who takes the place of Charmides, distinguishes in his answer between 'making' and 'doing,' and with the help of a misapplied quotation from Hesiod assigns to the words 'doing' and 'work' an exclusively good sense: Temperance is doing one's own business;--(4) is doing good.

Still an element of knowledge is wanting which Critias is readily induced to admit at the suggestion of Socrates; and, in the spirit of Socrates and of Greek life generally, proposes as a fifth definition, (5) Temperance is self-knowledge. But all sciences have a subject: number is the subject of arithmetic, health of medicine--what is the subject of temperance or wisdom? The answer is that (6) Temperance is the knowledge of what a man knows and of what he does not know. But this is contrary to analogy; there is no vision of vision, but only of visible things; no love of loves, but only of beautiful things; how then can there be a knowledge of knowledge? That which is older, heavier, lighter, is older, heavier, and lighter than something else, not than itself, and this seems to be true of all relative notions--the object of relation is outside of them; at any rate they can only have relation to themselves in the form of that object. Whether there are any such cases of reflex relation or not, and whether that sort of knowledge which we term Temperance is of this reflex nature, has yet to be determined by the great metaphysician. But even if knowledge can know itself, how does the knowledge of what we know imply the knowledge of what we do not know? Besides, knowledge is an abstraction only, and will not inform us of any particular subject, such as medicine, building, and the like. It may tell us that we or other men know something, but can never tell us what we know.

Admitting that there is a knowledge of what we know and of what we do not know, which would supply a rule and measure of all things, still there would be no good in this; and the knowledge which temperance gives must be of a kind which will do us good; for temperance is a good. But this universal knowledge does not tend to our happiness and good: the only kind of knowledge which brings happiness is the knowledge of good and evil. To this Critias replies that the science or knowledge of good and evil, and all the other sciences, are regulated by the higher science or knowledge of knowledge. Socrates replies by again dividing the abstract from the concrete, and asks how this knowledge conduces to happiness in the same definite way in which medicine conduces to health.

And now, after making all these concessions, which are really inadmissible, we are still as far as ever from ascertaining the nature of temperance, which Charmides has already discovered, and had therefore better rest in the knowledge that the more temperate he is the happier he will be, and not trouble himself with the speculations of Socrates.

In this Dialogue may be noted (1) The Greek ideal of beauty and goodness, the vision of the fair soul in the fair body, realised in the beautiful Charmides; (2) The true conception of medicine as a science of the whole as well as the parts, and of the mind as well as the body, which is playfully intimated in the story of the Thracian; (3) The tendency of the age to verbal distinctions, which here, as in the Protagoras and Cratylus, are ascribed to the ingenuity of Prodicus; and to interpretations or rather parodies of Homer or Hesiod, which are eminently characteristic of Plato and his contemporaries; (4) The germ of an ethical principle contained in the notion that temperance is 'doing one's own business,' which in the Republic (such is the shifting character of the Platonic philosophy) is given as the definition, not of temperance, but of justice; (5) The impatience which is exhibited by Socrates of any definition of temperance in which an element of science or knowledge is not included; (6) The beginning of metaphysics and logic implied in the two questions: whether there can be a science of science, and whether the knowledge of what you know is the same as the knowledge of what you do not know; and also in the distinction between 'what you know' and 'that you know,' (Greek;) here too is the first conception of an absolute self-determined science (the claims of which, however, are disputed by Socrates, who asks cui bono?) as well as the first suggestion of the difficulty of the abstract and concrete, and one of the earliest anticipa-

tions of the relation of subject and object, and of the subjective element in knowledge--a 'rich banquet' of metaphysical
questions in which we 'taste of many things.' (7) And still
the mind of Plato, having snatched for a moment at these
shadows of the future, quickly rejects them: thus early has
he reached the conclusion that there can be no science which
is a 'science of nothing' (Parmen.). (8) The conception of a science of good and evil also first occurs here, an anticipation of
the Philebus and Republic as well as of moral philosophy in
later ages.

The dramatic interest of the Dialogue chiefly centres in
the youth Charmides, with whom Socrates talks in the kindly spirit of an elder. His childlike simplicity and ingenuous-
ness are contrasted with the dialectical and rhetorical arts
of Critias, who is the grown-up man of the world, having a
tincture of philosophy. No hint is given, either here or in the
Timaeus, of the infamy which attaches to the name of the
latter in Athenian history. He is simply a cultivated person
who, like his kinsman Plato, is ennobled by the connection
of his family with Solon (Tim.), and had been the follower,
if not the disciple, both of Socrates and of the Sophists. In
the argument he is not unfair, if allowance is made for a
slight rhetorical tendency, and for a natural desire to save
his reputation with the company; he is sometimes nearer the
truth than Socrates. Nothing in his language or behaviour
is unbecoming the guardian of the beautiful Charmides. His
love of reputation is characteristically Greek, and contrasts
with the humility of Socrates. Nor in Charmides himself
do we find any resemblance to the Charmides of history,
except, perhaps, the modest and retiring nature which, according to Xenophon, at one time of his life prevented him
from speaking in the Assembly (Mem.); and we are surprised
to hear that, like Critias, he afterwards became one of the
thirty tyrants. In the Dialogue he is a pattern of virtue, and
is therefore in no need of the charm which Socrates is unable to apply. With youthful naivete, keeping his secret and
entering into the spirit of Socrates, he enjoys the detection
of his elder and guardian Critias, who is easily seen to be
the author of the definition which he has so great an inter-

est in maintaining. The preceding definition, 'Temperance is doing one's own business,' is assumed to have been borrowed by Charmides from another; and when the enquiry becomes more abstract he is superseded by Critias (Theaet.; Euthyd.). Socrates preserves his accustomed irony to the end; he is in the neighbourhood of several great truths, which he views in various lights, but always either by bringing them to the test of common sense, or by demanding too great exactness in the use of words, turns aside from them and comes at last to no conclusion.

The definitions of temperance proceed in regular order from the popular to the philosophical. The first two are simple enough and partially true, like the first thoughts of an intelligent youth; the third, which is a real contribution to ethical philosophy, is perverted by the ingenuity of Socrates, and hardly rescued by an equal perversion on the part of Critias. The remaining definitions have a higher aim, which is to introduce the element of knowledge, and at last to unite good and truth in a single science. But the time has not yet arrived for the realization of this vision of metaphysical philosophy; and such a science when brought nearer to us in the Philebus and the Republic will not be called by the name of (Greek). Hence we see with surprise that Plato, who in his other writings identifies good and knowledge, here opposes them, and asks, almost in the spirit of Aristotle, how can there be a knowledge of knowledge, and even if attainable, how can such a knowledge be of any use?

The difficulty of the Charmides arises chiefly from the two senses of the word (Greek), or temperance. From the ethical notion of temperance, which is variously defined to be quietness, modesty, doing our own business, the doing of good actions, the dialogue passes onto the intellectual conception of (Greek), which is declared also to be the science of self-knowledge, or of the knowledge of what we know and do not know, or of the knowledge of good and evil. The dialogue represents a stage in the history of philosophy in which knowledge and action were not yet distinguished. Hence the confusion between them, and the easy transition from one to the other. The definitions which are offered are all rejected, but it is to be observed that they all tend to throw a light on the nature of temperance, and that, unlike the distinction of Critias between (Greek), none of them are merely verbal quibbles, it is implied that this question, although it has not yet received a solution in theory, has been already answered by Charmides himself, who has learned to practise the virtue of self-knowledge which philosophers are vainly trying to define in words. In a similar spirit we might say to a young man who is disturbed by theological difficulties, 'Do not trouble yourself about such matters, but only lead a good life;' and yet in either case it is not to be denied that right ideas of truth may contribute greatly to the improvement of character.

The reasons why the Charmides, Lysis, Laches have been placed together and first in the series of Platonic dialogues, are: (i) Their shortness and simplicity. The Charmides and the Lysis, if not the Laches, are of the same 'quality' as the Phaedrus and Symposium: and it is probable, though far from certain, that the slighter effort preceded the greater one. (ii) Their eristic, or rather Socratic character; they belong to the class called dialogues of search (Greek), which have no conclusion. (iii) The absence in them of certain favourite notions of Plato, such as the doctrine of recollection and of the Platonic ideas; the questions, whether virtue can be taught; whether the virtues are one or many. (iv) They have a want of depth, when compared with the dialogues of the middle and later period; and a youthful beauty and grace which is wanting in the later ones. (v) Their resemblance to one another; in all the three boyhood has a great part. These reasons have various degrees of weight in determining their place in the catalogue of the Platonic writings, though they are not conclusive. No arrangement of the Platonic dialogues can be strictly chronological. The order which has been adopted is intended mainly for the convenience of the reader; at the same time, indications of the date supplied either by Plato himself or allusions found in the dialogues have not been lost sight of. Much may be said about this subject, but the results can only be probable; there are no materials which would enable us to attain to anything like certainty.

The relations of knowledge and virtue are again brought forward in the companion dialogues of the Lysis and Laches; and also in the Protagoras and Euthydemus. The opposition of abstract and particular knowledge in this dialogue may be compared with a similar opposition of ideas and phenomena which occurs in the Prologues to the Parmenides, but seems rather to belong to a later stage of the philosophy of Plato.

CHARMIDES, OR TEMPERANCE

PERSONS OF THE DIALOGUE:

Socrates, who is the narrator,

Charmides,

Chaerephon,

Critias.

SCENE: The Palaestra of Taureas, which is near the Porch of the King Archon.

Yesterday evening I returned from the army at Potidaea, and having been a good while away, I thought that I should like to go and look at my old haunts. So I went into the palaestra of Taureas, which is over against the temple adjoining the porch of the King Archon, and there I found a number of persons, most of whom I knew, but not all. My visit was unexpected, and no sooner did they see me entering than they saluted me from afar on all sides; and Chaerephon, who is a kind of madman, started up and ran to me, seizing my hand, and saying, How did you escape, Socrates?--(I should explain that an engagement had taken place at Potidaea not long before we came away, of which the news had only just reached Athens.)

You see, I replied, that here I am.

There was a report, he said, that the engagement was very severe, and that many of our acquaintance had fallen.

That, I replied, was not far from the truth.

I suppose, he said, that you were present.

I was.

Then sit down, and tell us the whole story, which as yet we have only heard imperfectly.

I took the place which he assigned to me, by the side of Critias the son of Callaeschrus, and when I had saluted him and the rest of the company, I told them the news from the army, and answered their several enquiries.

Then, when there had been enough of this, I, in my turn, began to make enquiries about matters at home--about the present state of philosophy, and about the youth. I asked whether any of them were remarkable for wisdom or beauty, or both. Critias, glancing at the door, invited my attention to some youths who were coming in, and talking noisily to one another, followed by a crowd. Of the beauties, Socrates, he said, I fancy that you will soon be able to form a judgment. For those who are just entering are the advanced guard of the great beauty, as he is thought to be, of the day, and he is likely to be not far off himself.

Who is he, I said; and who is his father?

Charmides, he replied, is his name; he is my cousin, and
the son of my uncle Glaucon: I rather think that you know
him too, although he was not grown up at the time of your
departure.

Certainly, I know him, I said, for he was remarkable even
then when he was still a child, and I should imagine that by
this time he must be almost a young man.

You will see, he said, in a moment what progress he has
made and what he is like. He had scarcely said the word,
when Charmides entered.

Now you know, my friend, that I cannot measure anything, and of the beautiful, I am simply such a measure as a
white line is of chalk; for almost all young persons appear to
be beautiful in my eyes. But at that moment, when I saw him
coming in, I confess that I was quite astonished at his beauty
and stature; all the world seemed to be enamoured of him;
amazement and confusion reigned when he entered; and a
troop of lovers followed him. That grown-up men like ourselves should have been affected in this way was not surpris-
ing, but I observed that there was the same feeling among
the boys; all of them, down to the very least child, turned and
looked at him, as if he had been a statue.

Chaerephon called me and said: What do you think of
him, Socrates? Has he not a beautiful face?

Most beautiful, I said.

But you would think nothing of his face, he replied, if you
could see his naked form: he is absolutely perfect.

And to this they all agreed.

By Heracles, I said, there never was such a paragon, if he
has only one other slight addition.

What is that? said Critias.

If he has a noble soul; and being of your house, Critias, he may be expected to have this.

He is as fair and good within, as he is without, replied Critias.

Then, before we see his body, should we not ask him to show us his soul, naked and undisguised? he is just of an age at which he will like to talk.

That he will, said Critias, and I can tell you that he is a philosopher already, and also a considerable poet, not in his own opinion only, but in that of others.

That, my dear Critias, I replied, is a distinction which has long been in your family, and is inherited by you from Solon. But why do you not call him, and show him to us? for even if he were younger than he is, there could be no impropriety in his talking to us in the presence of you, who are his guardian and cousin.

Very well, he said; then I will call him; and turning to the attendant, he said, Call Charmides, and tell him that I want him to come and see a physician about the illness of which he spoke to me the day before yesterday. Then again addressing me, he added: He has been complaining lately of having a headache when he rises in the morning: now why should you not make him believe that you know a cure for the headache?

Why not, I said; but will he come?

He will be sure to come, he replied.

He came as he was bidden, and sat down between Critias and me. Great amusement was occasioned by every one pushing with might and main at his neighbour in order to make a place for him next to themselves, until at the two ends of the row one had to get up and the other was rolled over sideways. Now I, my friend, was beginning to feel awkward; my former bold belief in my powers of conversing with him had vanished. And when Critias told him that I was the person who had the cure, he looked at me in such an indescribable manner, and was just going to ask a question. And at that moment all the people in the palaestra crowded about us, and, O rare! I caught a sight of the inwards of his garment, and took the flame. Then I could no longer contain myself. I thought how well Cydias understood the nature of love, when, in speaking of a fair youth, he warns some one 'not to bring the fawn in the sight of the lion to be devoured by him,' for I felt that I had been overcome by a sort of wild-beast appetite. But I controlled myself, and when he asked me if I knew the cure of the headache, I answered, but with an effort, that I did know.

And what is it? he said.

I replied that it was a kind of leaf, which required to be accompanied by a charm, and if a person would repeat the charm at the same time that he used the cure, he would be made whole; but that without the charm the leaf would be of no avail.

Then I will write out the charm from your dictation, he said.

With my consent? I said, or without my consent?

With your consent, Socrates, he said, laughing.

Very good, I said; and are you quite sure that you know my name?

I ought to know you, he replied, for there is a great deal said about you among my companions; and I remember when I was a child seeing you in company with my cousin Critias.

I am glad to find that you remember me, I said; for I shall now be more at home with you and shall be better able to explain the nature of the charm, about which I felt a difficulty before. For the charm will do more, Charmides, than only cure the headache. I dare say that you have heard eminent physicians say to a patient who comes to them with bad eyes, that they cannot cure his eyes by themselves, but that if his eyes are to be cured, his head must be treated; and then again they say that to think of curing the head alone, and not the rest of the body also, is the height of folly. And arguing in this way they apply their methods to the whole body, and try to treat and heal the whole and the part together. Did you ever observe that this is what they say?

Yes, he said.

And they are right, and you would agree with them?

Yes, he said, certainly I should.

His approving answers reassured me, and I began by degrees to regain confidence, and the vital heat returned. Such, Charmides, I said, is the nature of the charm, which I learned when serving with the army from one of the physicians of the Thracian king Zamolxis, who are said to be so skilful that they can even give immortality. This Thracian told me that in these notions of theirs, which I was just now mentioning, the Greek physicians are quite right as far as they go; but Zamolxis, he added, our king, who is also a god, says further, 'that as you ought not to attempt to cure the eyes without the head, or the head without the body, so neither ought you to attempt to cure the body without the soul; and this,' he said, 'is the reason why the cure of many diseases is unknown to the physicians of Hellas, because they are ignorant of the whole, which ought to be studied also; for the part can never be well unless the whole is well.' For all good and evil, whether in the body or in human nature, originates, as he declared, in the soul, and overflows from thence, as if from the head into the eyes. And therefore if the head and body are to be well, you must begin by curing the soul; that is the first thing. And the cure, my dear youth, has to be effected by the use of certain charms, and these charms are fair words; and by them temperance is implanted in the soul, and where temperance is, there health is speedily imparted, not only to the head, but to the whole body. And he who taught me the cure and the charm at the same time added a special direction: 'Let no one,' he said, 'persuade you to cure the head, until he has first given you his soul to be cured by the charm. For this,' he said, 'is the great error of our day in the treatment of the human body, that physicians separate the soul from the body.'

And he added with emphasis, at the same time making me swear to his words, 'Let no one, however rich, or noble, or fair, persuade you to give him the cure, without the charm.' Now I have sworn, and I must keep my oath, and therefore if you will allow me to apply the Thracian charm first to your soul, as the stranger directed, I will afterwards proceed to apply the cure to your head. But if not, I do not know what I am to do with you, my dear Charmides.

Critias, when he heard this, said: The headache will be an unexpected gain to my young relation, if the pain in his head compels him to improve his mind: and I can tell you, Socrates, that Charmides is not only pre-eminent in beauty among his equals, but also in that quality which is given by the charm; and this, as you say, is temperance?

Yes, I said.

Then let me tell you that he is the most temperate of human beings, and for his age inferior to none in any quality.

Yes, I said, Charmides; and indeed I think that you ought to excel others in all good qualities; for if I am not mistaken there is no one present who could easily point out two Athenian houses, whose union would be likely to produce a better or nobler scion than the two from which you are sprung. There is your father's house, which is descended from Critias the son of Dropidas, whose family has been commemorated in the panegyrical verses of Anacreon, Solon, and many other poets, as famous for beauty and virtue and all other high fortune: and your mother's house is equally distinguished; for your maternal uncle, Pyrilampes, is reputed never to have found his equal, in Persia at the court of the great king, or on the continent of Asia, in all the places to which he went as ambassador, for stature and beauty; that whole family is not a whit inferior to the other. Having such ancestors you ought to be first in all things, and, sweet son of Glaucon, your outward form is no dishonour to any of them. If to beauty you add temperance, and if in other respects you are what Critias declares you to be, then, dear Charmides, blessed art thou, in being the son of thy mother. And here lies the point; for if,

as he declares, you have this gift of temperance already, and
are temperate enough, in that case you have no need of any
charms, whether of Zamolxis or of Abaris the Hyperborean,
and I may as well let you have the cure of the head at once;
but if you have not yet acquired this quality, I must use the
charm before I give you the medicine. Please, therefore, to
inform me whether you admit the truth of what Critias has
been saying;--have you or have you not this quality of temperance?

Charmides blushed, and the blush heightened his beauty,
for modesty is becoming in youth; he then said very ingenu-
ously, that he really could not at once answer, either yes, or
no, to the question which I had asked: For, said he, if I affirm
that I am not temperate, that would be a strange thing for
me to say of myself, and also I should give the lie to Critias,
and many others who think as he tells you, that I am temperate: but, on the other hand, if I say that I am, I shall have to
praise myself, which would be ill manners; and therefore I do
not know how to answer you.

I said to him: That is a natural reply, Charmides, and I
think that you and I ought together to enquire whether you
have this quality about which I am asking or not; and then
you will not be compelled to say what you do not like; neither
shall I be a rash practitioner of medicine: therefore, if you
please, I will share the enquiry with you, but I will not press
you if you would rather not.

There is nothing which I should like better, he said; and
as far as I am concerned you may proceed in the way which
you think best.

I think, I said, that I had better begin by asking you a
question; for if temperance abides in you, you must have an
opinion about her; she must give some intimation of her nature and qualities, which may enable you to form a notion of
her. Is not that true?

Yes, he said, that I think is true.

You know your native language, I said, and therefore you

must be able to tell what you feel about this.

Certainly, he said.

In order, then, that I may form a conjecture whether you have temperance abiding in you or not, tell me, I said, what, in your opinion, is Temperance?

At first he hesitated, and was very unwilling to answer: then he said that he thought temperance was doing things orderly and quietly, such things for example as walking in the streets, and talking, or anything else of that nature. In a word, he said, I should answer that, in my opinion, temperance is quietness.

Are you right, Charmides? I said. No doubt some would affirm that the quiet are the temperate; but let us see whether these words have any meaning; and first tell me whether you would not acknowledge temperance to be of the class of the noble and good?

Yes.

But which is best when you are at the writing-master's, to write the same letters quickly or quietly?

Quickly.

And to read quickly or slowly?

Quickly again.

And in playing the lyre, or wrestling, quickness or sharpness are far better than quietness and slowness?

Yes.

And the same holds in boxing and in the pancratium?

Certainly.

And in leaping and running and in bodily exercises generally, quickness and agility are good; slowness, and inactivity, and quietness, are bad?

That is evident.

Then, I said, in all bodily actions, not quietness, but the greatest agility and quickness, is noblest and best?

Yes, certainly.

And is temperance a good?

Yes.

Then, in reference to the body, not quietness, but quickness will be the higher degree of temperance, if temperance is a good?

True, he said.

And which, I said, is better--facility in learning, or difficulty in learning?

Facility.

Yes, I said; and facility in learning is learning quickly, and difficulty in learning is learning quietly and slowly?

True.

And is it not better to teach another quickly and energetically, rather than quietly and slowly?

Yes.

And which is better, to call to mind, and to remember, quickly and readily, or quietly and slowly?

The former.

And is not shrewdness a quickness or cleverness of the soul, and not a quietness?

True.

And is it not best to understand what is said, whether at the writing-master's or the music-master's, or anywhere else, not as quietly as possible, but as quickly as possible?

Yes.

And in the searchings or deliberations of the soul, not the quietest, as I imagine, and he who with difficulty deliberates and discovers, is thought worthy of praise, but he who does so most easily and quickly?

Quite true, he said.

And in all that concerns either body or soul, swiftness and activity are clearly better than slowness and quietness?

Clearly they are.

Then temperance is not quietness, nor is the temperate life quiet,--certainly not upon this view; for the life which is temperate is supposed to be the good. And of two things, one is true,--either never, or very seldom, do the quiet actions in life appear to be better than the quick and energetic ones; or supposing that of the nobler actions, there are as many quiet, as quick and vehement: still, even if we grant this, temperance will not be acting quietly any more than acting quickly and energetically, either in walking or talking or in anything else; nor will the quiet life be more temperate than the unquiet, seeing that temperance is admitted by us to be a good and noble thing, and the quick have been shown to be as good as the quiet.

I think, he said, Socrates, that you are right.

Then once more, Charmides, I said, fix your attention, and look within; consider the effect which temperance has upon yourself, and the nature of that which has the effect. Think over all this, and, like a brave youth, tell me--What is temperance?

After a moment's pause, in which he made a real manly effort to think, he said: My opinion is, Socrates, that temperance makes a man ashamed or modest, and that temperance is the same as modesty.

Very good, I said; and did you not admit, just now, that temperance is noble?

Yes, certainly, he said.

And the temperate are also good?

Yes.

And can that be good which does not make men good?

Certainly not.

And you would infer that temperance is not only noble, but also good?

That is my opinion.

Well, I said; but surely you would agree with Homer when he says,

'Modesty is not good for a needy man'?

Yes, he said; I agree.

Then I suppose that modesty is and is not good?

Clearly.

But temperance, whose presence makes men only good, and not bad, is always good?

That appears to me to be as you say.

And the inference is that temperance cannot be modesty- -if temperance is a good, and if modesty is as much an evil as a good?

All that, Socrates, appears to me to be true; but I should like to know what you think about another definition of temperance, which I just now remember to have heard from some one, who said, 'That temperance is doing our own business.' Was he right who affirmed that?

You monster! I said; this is what Critias, or some philosopher has told you.

Some one else, then, said Critias; for certainly I have not.

But what matter, said Charmides, from whom I heard

this?

No matter at all, I replied; for the point is not who said the words, but whether they are true or not.

There you are in the right, Socrates, he replied.

To be sure, I said; yet I doubt whether we shall ever be able to discover their truth or falsehood; for they are a kind of riddle.

What makes you think so? he said.

Because, I said, he who uttered them seems to me to have meant one thing, and said another. Is the scribe, for example, to be regarded as doing nothing when he reads or writes?

I should rather think that he was doing something.

And does the scribe write or read, or teach you boys to write or read, your own names only, or did you write your enemies' names as well as your own and your friends'?

As much one as the other.

And was there anything meddling or intemperate in this?

Certainly not.

And yet if reading and writing are the same as doing, you were doing what was not your own business?

But they are the same as doing.

And the healing art, my friend, and building, and weaving, and doing anything whatever which is done by art,-- these all clearly come under the head of doing?

Certainly.

And do you think that a state would be well ordered by a law which compelled every man to weave and wash his own coat, and make his own shoes, and his own flask and strigil, and other implements, on this principle of every one doing and performing his own, and abstaining from what is not his own?

I think not, he said.

But, I said, a temperate state will be a well-ordered state.

Of course, he replied.

Then temperance, I said, will not be doing one's own business; not at least in this way, or doing things of this sort?

Clearly not.

Then, as I was just now saying, he who declared that temperance is a man doing his own business had another and a hidden meaning; for I do not think that he could have been such a fool as to mean this. Was he a fool who told you, Charmides?

Nay, he replied, I certainly thought him a very wise man.

Then I am quite certain that he put forth his definition as a riddle, thinking that no one would know the meaning of the words 'doing his own business.'

I dare say, he replied.

And what is the meaning of a man doing his own business? Can you tell me?

Indeed, I cannot; and I should not wonder if the man himself who used this phrase did not understand what he was saying. Whereupon he laughed slyly, and looked at Critias.

Critias had long been showing uneasiness, for he felt that he had a reputation to maintain with Charmides and the rest of the company. He had, however, hitherto managed to restrain himself; but now he could no longer forbear, and I am convinced of the truth of the suspicion which I entertained at the time, that Charmides had heard this answer about temperance from Critias. And Charmides, who did not want to answer himself, but to make Critias answer, tried to stir him up. He went on pointing out that he had been refuted, at which Critias grew angry, and appeared, as I thought, inclined to quarrel with him; just as a poet might quarrel with an actor who spoiled his poems in repeating them; so he looked hard at him and said--

Do you imagine, Charmides, that the author of this definition of temperance did not understand the meaning of his own words, because you do not understand them?

Why, at his age, I said, most excellent Critias, he can hardly be expected to understand; but you, who are older, and have studied, may well be assumed to know the meaning of them; and therefore, if you agree with him, and accept his definition of temperance, I would much rather argue with you than with him about the truth or falsehood of the definition.

I entirely agree, said Critias, and accept the definition.

Very good, I said; and now let me repeat my question--Do you admit, as I was just now saying, that all craftsmen make or do something?

I do.

And do they make or do their own business only, or that of others also?

They make or do that of others also.

And are they temperate, seeing that they make not for themselves or their own business only?

Why not? he said.

No objection on my part, I said, but there may be a difficulty on his who proposes as a definition of temperance, 'doing one's own business,' and then says that there is no reason why those who do the business of others should not be temperate.

Nay (The English reader has to observe that the word

'make' (Greek), in Greek, has also the sense of 'do' (Greek).), said he; did I ever acknowledge that those who do the business of others are temperate? I said, those who make, not those who do.

What! I asked; do you mean to say that doing and making are not the same?

No more, he replied, than making or working are the same; thus much I have learned from Hesiod, who says that 'work is no disgrace.' Now do you imagine that if he had meant by working and doing such things as you were describing, he would have said that there was no disgrace in them--for example, in the manufacture of shoes, or in selling pickles, or sitting for hire in a house of ill-fame? That, Socrates, is not to be supposed: but I conceive him to have distinguished making from doing and work; and, while admitting that the making anything might sometimes become a disgrace, when the employment was not honourable, to have thought that work was never any disgrace at all. For things nobly and usefully made he called works; and such makings he called workings, and doings; and he must be supposed to have called such things only man's proper business, and what is hurtful, not his business: and in that sense Hesiod, and any other wise man, may be reasonably supposed to call him wise who does his own work.

O Critias, I said, no sooner had you opened your mouth, than I pretty well knew that you would call that which is proper to a man, and that which is his own, good; and that the makings (Greek) of the good you would call doings (Greek), for I am no stranger to the endless distinctions which Prodicus draws about names. Now I have no objection to your giving names any signification which you please, if you will only tell me what you mean by them. Please then to begin again, and be a little plainer. Do you mean that this doing or making, or whatever is the word which you would use, of good actions, is temperance?

I do, he said.

Then not he who does evil, but he who does good, is temperate?

Yes, he said; and you, friend, would agree.

No matter whether I should or not; just now, not what I think, but what you are saying, is the point at issue.

Well, he answered; I mean to say, that he who does evil, and not good, is not temperate; and that he is temperate who does good, and not evil: for temperance I define in plain words to be the doing of good actions.

And you may be very likely right in what you are saying; but I am curious to know whether you imagine that temperate men are ignorant of their own temperance?

I do not think so, he said.

And yet were you not saying, just now, that craftsmen might be temperate in doing another's work, as well as in doing their own?

I was, he replied; but what is your drift?

I have no particular drift, but I wish that you would tell me whether a physician who cures a patient may do good to himself and good to another also?

I think that he may.

And he who does so does his duty?

Yes.

And does not he who does his duty act temperately or wisely?

Yes, he acts wisely.

But must the physician necessarily know when his treatment is likely to prove beneficial, and when not? or must the craftsman necessarily know when he is likely to be benefited, and when not to be benefited, by the work which he is doing?

I suppose not.

Then, I said, he may sometimes do good or harm, and not know what he is himself doing, and yet, in doing good, as you say, he has done temperately or wisely. Was not that your statement?

Yes.

Then, as would seem, in doing good, he may act wisely or temperately, and be wise or temperate, but not know his own wisdom or temperance?

But that, Socrates, he said, is impossible; and therefore if this is, as you imply, the necessary consequence of any of my previous admissions, I will withdraw them, rather than admit that a man can be temperate or wise who does not know himself; and I am not ashamed to confess that I was in error. For self-knowledge would certainly be maintained by me to be the very essence of knowledge, and in this I agree with him who dedicated the inscription, 'Know thyself!' at Delphi. That word, if I am not mistaken, is put there as a sort of salutation which the god addresses to those who enter the temple; as much as to say that the ordinary salutation of 'Hail!' is not right, and that the exhortation 'Be temperate!' would be a far better way of saluting one another. The notion of him who dedicated the inscription was, as I believe, that the god speaks to those who enter his temple, not as men speak; but, when a worshipper enters, the first word which he hears is 'Be temperate!' This, however, like a prophet he expresses in a sort of riddle, for 'Know thyself!' and 'Be temperate!' are the same, as I maintain, and as the letters imply (Greek), and yet they may be easily misunderstood; and succeeding sages who added 'Never too much,' or, 'Give a pledge, and evil is nigh at hand,' would appear to have so misunderstood them; for they imagined that 'Know thyself!' was a piece of advice which the god gave, and not his salutation of the worshippers at their first coming in; and they dedicated their own inscription under the idea that they too would give equally useful pieces of advice. Shall I tell you, Socrates, why I say all this? My object is to leave the previous discussion (in which I know not whether you or I are more right, but, at any rate, no clear result was attained), and to raise a new one in which I will attempt to prove, if you deny, that temperance is self-knowledge.

Yes, I said, Critias; but you come to me as though I professed to know about the questions which I ask, and as though I could, if I only would, agree with you. Whereas the fact is that I enquire with you into the truth of that which is advanced from time to time, just because I do not know; and when I have enquired, I will say whether I agree with you or not. Please then to allow me time to reflect.

Reflect, he said.

I am reflecting, I replied, and discover that temperance, or wisdom, if implying a knowledge of anything, must be a science, and a science of something.

Yes, he said; the science of itself.

Is not medicine, I said, the science of health?

True.

And suppose, I said, that I were asked by you what is the use or effect of medicine, which is this science of health, I should answer that medicine is of very great use in producing health, which, as you will admit, is an excellent effect.

Granted.

And if you were to ask me, what is the result or effect of architecture, which is the science of building, I should say houses, and so of other arts, which all have their different results. Now I want you, Critias, to answer a similar question about temperance, or wisdom, which, according to you, is the science of itself. Admitting this view, I ask of you, what good work, worthy of the name wise, does temperance or wisdom, which is the science of itself, effect? Answer me.

That is not the true way of pursuing the enquiry, Socrates, he said; for wisdom is not like the other sciences, any

more than they are like one another: but you proceed as if
they were alike. For tell me, he said, what result is there of
computation or geometry, in the same sense as a house is
the result of building, or a garment of weaving, or any other
work of any other art? Can you show me any such result of
them? You cannot.

That is true, I said; but still each of these sciences has a
subject which is different from the science. I can show you
that the art of computation has to do with odd and even numbers in their numerical relations to themselves and to each
other. Is not that true?

Yes, he said.

And the odd and even numbers are not the same with the
art of computation?

They are not.

The art of weighing, again, has to do with lighter and
heavier; but the art of weighing is one thing, and the heavy
and the light another. Do you admit that?

Yes.

Now, I want to know, what is that which is not wisdom,
and of which wisdom is the science?

You are just falling into the old error, Socrates, he said.
You come asking in what wisdom or temperance differs from
the other sciences, and then you try to discover some respect
in which they are alike; but they are not, for all the other sciences are of something else, and not of themselves; wisdom
alone is a science of other sciences, and of itself. And of this,
as I believe, you are very well aware: and that you are only
doing what you denied that you were doing just now, trying
to refute me, instead of pursuing the argument.

And what if I am? How can you think that I have any
other motive in refuting you but what I should have in examining into myself? which motive would be just a fear of my
unconsciously fancying that I knew something of which I was

ignorant. And at this moment I pursue the argument chiefly for my own sake, and perhaps in some degree also for the sake of my other friends. For is not the discovery of things as they truly are, a good common to all mankind?

Yes, certainly, Socrates, he said.

Then, I said, be cheerful, sweet sir, and give your opinion in answer to the question which I asked, never minding whether Critias or Socrates is the person refuted; attend only to the argument, and see what will come of the refutation.

I think that you are right, he replied; and I will do as you say.

Tell me, then, I said, what you mean to affirm about wisdom.

I mean to say that wisdom is the only science which is the science of itself as well as of the other sciences.

But the science of science, I said, will also be the science of the absence of science.

Very true, he said.

Then the wise or temperate man, and he only, will know himself, and be able to examine what he knows or does not know, and to see what others know and think that they know and do really know; and what they do not know, and fancy that they know, when they do not. No other person will be able to do this. And this is wisdom and temperance and self-knowledge--for a man to know what he knows, and what he does not know. That is your meaning?

Yes, he said.

Now then, I said, making an offering of the third or last argument to Zeus the Saviour, let us begin again, and ask, in the first place, whether it is or is not possible for a person to know that he knows and does not know what he knows and does not know; and in the second place, whether, if perfectly possible, such knowledge is of any use.

That is what we have to consider, he said.

And here, Critias, I said, I hope that you will find a way out of a difficulty into which I have got myself. Shall I tell you the nature of the difficulty?

By all means, he replied.

Does not what you have been saying, if true, amount to this: that there must be a single science which is wholly a science of itself and of other sciences, and that the same is also the science of the absence of science?

Yes.

But consider how monstrous this proposition is, my friend: in any parallel case, the impossibility will be transparent to you.

How is that? and in what cases do you mean?

In such cases as this: Suppose that there is a kind of vision which is not like ordinary vision, but a vision of itself and of other sorts of vision, and of the defect of them, which in seeing sees no colour, but only itself and other sorts of vision: Do you think that there is such a kind of vision?

Certainly not.

Or is there a kind of hearing which hears no sound at all, but only itself and other sorts of hearing, or the defects of them?

There is not.

Or take all the senses: can you imagine that there is any sense of itself and of other senses, but which is incapable of perceiving the objects of the senses?

I think not.

Could there be any desire which is not the desire of any pleasure, but of itself, and of all other desires?

Certainly not.

Or can you imagine a wish which wishes for no good, but only for itself and all other wishes?

I should answer, No.

Or would you say that there is a love which is not the love of beauty, but of itself and of other loves?

I should not.

Or did you ever know of a fear which fears itself or other fears, but has no object of fear?

I never did, he said.

Or of an opinion which is an opinion of itself and of other opinions, and which has no opinion on the subjects of opinion in general?

Certainly not.

But surely we are assuming a science of this kind, which, having no subject-matter, is a science of itself and of the other sciences?

Yes, that is what is affirmed.

But how strange is this, if it be indeed true: we must not however as yet absolutely deny the possibility of such a science; let us rather consider the matter.

You are quite right.

Well then, this science of which we are speaking is a science of something, and is of a nature to be a science of something?

Yes.

Just as that which is greater is of a nature to be greater than something else? (Socrates is intending to show that science differs from the object of science, as any other relative differs from the object of relation. But where there is comparison--greater, less, heavier, lighter, and the like--a relation to self as well as to other things involves an absolute contradiction; and in other cases, as in the case of the senses, is hardly conceivable. The use of the genitive after the comparative in Greek, (Greek), creates an unavoidable obscurity in the translation.)

Yes.

Which is less, if the other is conceived to be greater?

To be sure.

And if we could find something which is at once greater than itself, and greater than other great things, but not greater than those things in comparison of which the others are greater, then that thing would have the property of being greater and also less than itself?

That, Socrates, he said, is the inevitable inference.

Or if there be a double which is double of itself and of other doubles, these will be halves; for the double is relative to the half?

That is true.

And that which is greater than itself will also be less, and that which is heavier will also be lighter, and that which is older will also be younger: and the same of other things; that which has a nature relative to self will retain also the nature of its object: I mean to say, for example, that hearing is, as we say, of sound or voice. Is that true?

Yes.

Then if hearing hears itself, it must hear a voice; for there is no other way of hearing.

Certainly.

And sight also, my excellent friend, if it sees itself must see a colour, for sight cannot see that which has no colour.

No.

Do you remark, Critias, that in several of the examples

which have been recited the notion of a relation to self is altogether inadmissible, and in other cases hardly credible- -inadmissible, for example, in the case of magnitudes, numbers, and the like?

Very true.

But in the case of hearing and sight, or in the power of self-motion, and the power of heat to burn, this relation to self will be regarded as incredible by some, but perhaps not by others. And some great man, my friend, is wanted, who will satisfactorily determine for us, whether there is nothing which has an inherent property of relation to self, or some things only and not others; and whether in this class of self-related things, if there be such a class, that science which is called wisdom or temperance is included. I altogether distrust my own power of determining these matters: I am not certain whether there is such a science of science at all; and even if there be, I should not acknowledge this to be wisdom or temperance, until I can also see whether such a science would or would not do us any good; for I have an impression that temperance is a benefit and a good. And therefore, O son of Callaeschrus, as you maintain that temperance or wisdom is a science of science, and also of the absence of science, I will request you to show in the first place, as I was saying before, the possibility, and in the second place, the advantage, of such a science; and then perhaps you may satisfy me that you are right in your view of temperance.

Critias heard me say this, and saw that I was in a difficulty; and as one person when another yawns in his presence catches the infection of yawning from him, so did he seem to be driven into a difficulty by my difficulty. But as he had a reputation to maintain, he was ashamed to admit before the company that he could not answer my challenge or determine the question at issue; and he made an unintelligible attempt to hide his perplexity. In order that the argument might proceed, I said to him, Well then Critias, if you like, let us assume that there is this science of science; whether the assumption is right or wrong may hereafter be investigated. Admitting the existence of it, will you tell me how such a science enables us to distinguish what we know or do not know, which, as we were saying, is self-knowledge or wisdom: so we were saying?

Yes, Socrates, he said; and that I think is certainly true: for he who has this science or knowledge which knows itself will become like the knowledge which he has, in the same way that he who has swiftness will be swift, and he who has beauty will be beautiful, and he who has knowledge will know. In the same way he who has that knowledge which is self-knowing, will know himself.

I do not doubt, I said, that a man will know himself, when he possesses that which has self-knowledge: but what necessity is there that, having this, he should know what he knows and what he does not know?

Because, Socrates, they are the same.

Very likely, I said; but I remain as stupid as ever; for still I fail to comprehend how this knowing what you know and do not know is the same as the knowledge of self.

What do you mean? he said.

This is what I mean, I replied: I will admit that there is a science of science;--can this do more than determine that of two things one is and the other is not science or knowledge?

No, just that.

But is knowledge or want of knowledge of health the same as knowledge or want of knowledge of justice?

Certainly not.

The one is medicine, and the other is politics; whereas that of which we are speaking is knowledge pure and simple.

Very true.

And if a man knows only, and has only knowledge of knowledge, and has no further knowledge of health and justice, the probability is that he will only know that he knows something, and has a certain knowledge, whether concerning himself or other men.

True.

Then how will this knowledge or science teach him to know what he knows? Say that he knows health;--not wisdom or temperance, but the art of medicine has taught it to him;--and he has learned harmony from the art of music, and building from the art of building,--neither, from wisdom or temperance: and the same of other things.

That is evident.

How will wisdom, regarded only as a knowledge of knowledge or science of science, ever teach him that he knows health, or that he knows building?

It is impossible.

Then he who is ignorant of these things will only know that he knows, but not what he knows?

True.

Then wisdom or being wise appears to be not the knowledge of the things which we do or do not know, but only the knowledge that we know or do not know?

That is the inference.

Then he who has this knowledge will not be able to examine whether a pretender knows or does not know that which he says that he knows: he will only know that he has a knowledge of some kind; but wisdom will not show him of what the knowledge is?

Plainly not.

Neither will he be able to distinguish the pretender in medicine from the true physician, nor between any other true and false professor of knowledge. Let us consider the matter in this way: If the wise man or any other man wants to distinguish the true physician from the false, how will he proceed? He will not talk to him about medicine; and that, as we were saying, is the only thing which the physician understands.

True.

And, on the other hand, the physician knows nothing of science, for this has been assumed to be the province of wisdom.

True.

And further, since medicine is science, we must infer that he does not know anything of medicine.

Exactly.

Then the wise man may indeed know that the physician has some kind of science or knowledge; but when he wants to discover the nature of this he will ask, What is the subject-matter? For the several sciences are distinguished not by the mere fact that they are sciences, but by the nature of their subjects. Is not that true?

Quite true.

And medicine is distinguished from other sciences as having the subject-matter of health and disease?

Yes.

And he who would enquire into the nature of medicine must pursue the enquiry into health and disease, and not into what is extraneous?

True.

And he who judges rightly will judge of the physician as a physician in what relates to these?

He will.

He will consider whether what he says is true, and whether what he does is right, in relation to health and disease?

He will.

But can any one attain the knowledge of either unless he have a knowledge of medicine?

He cannot.

No one at all, it would seem, except the physician can have this knowledge; and therefore not the wise man; he would have to be a physician as well as a wise man.

Very true.

Then, assuredly, wisdom or temperance, if only a science of science, and of the absence of science or knowledge, will not be able to distinguish the physician who knows from one who does not know but pretends or thinks that he knows, or any other professor of anything at all; like any other artist, he will only know his fellow in art or wisdom, and no one else.

That is evident, he said.

But then what profit, Critias, I said, is there any longer in wisdom or temperance which yet remains, if this is wisdom? If, indeed, as we were supposing at first, the wise man had been able to distinguish what he knew and did not know, and that he knew the one and did not know the other, and to recognize a similar faculty of discernment in others, there would certainly have been a great advantage in being wise; for then we should never have made a mistake, but have passed through life the unerring guides of ourselves and of those who are under us; and we should not have attempted to do what we did not know, but we should have found out those who knew, and have handed the business over to them and trusted in them; nor should we have allowed those who were under us to do anything which they were not likely to do well; and they would be likely to do well just that of which they had knowledge; and the house or state which was ordered or administered under the guidance of wisdom, and everything else of which wisdom was the lord, would have been well ordered; for truth guiding, and error having been eliminated, in all their doings, men would have done well, and would have been happy. Was not this, Critias, what we spoke of as the great advantage of wisdom--to know what is known and what is unknown to us?

Very true, he said.

And now you perceive, I said, that no such science is to be found anywhere.

I perceive, he said.

May we assume then, I said, that wisdom, viewed in this new light merely as a knowledge of knowledge and ignorance, has this advantage:--that he who possesses such knowledge will more easily learn anything which he learns; and that everything will be clearer to him, because, in addition to the knowledge of individuals, he sees the science, and this also will better enable him to test the knowledge which others have of what he knows himself; whereas the enquirer who is without this knowledge may be supposed to have a feebler and weaker insight? Are not these, my friend, the real advantages which are to be gained from wisdom? And are not we looking and seeking after something more than is to be found in her?

That is very likely, he said.

That is very likely, I said; and very likely, too, we have been enquiring to no purpose; as I am led to infer, because I observe that if this is wisdom, some strange consequences would follow. Let us, if you please, assume the possibility of this science of sciences, and further admit and allow, as was originally suggested, that wisdom is the knowledge of what we know and do not know. Assuming all this, still, upon further consideration, I am doubtful, Critias, whether wisdom, such as this, would do us much good. For we were wrong, I think, in supposing, as we were saying just now, that such wisdom ordering the government of house or state would be a great benefit.

How so? he said.

Why, I said, we were far too ready to admit the great benefits which mankind would obtain from their severally doing the things which they knew, and committing the things of which they are ignorant to those who were better acquainted with them.

Were we not right in making that admission?

I think not.

How very strange, Socrates!

By the dog of Egypt, I said, there I agree with you; and I was thinking as much just now when I said that strange consequences would follow, and that I was afraid we were on the wrong track; for however ready we may be to admit that this is wisdom, I certainly cannot make out what good this sort of thing does to us.

What do you mean? he said; I wish that you could make me understand what you mean.

I dare say that what I am saying is nonsense, I replied; and yet if a man has any feeling of what is due to himself, he cannot let the thought which comes into his mind pass away unheeded and unexamined.

I like that, he said.

Hear, then, I said, my own dream; whether coming through the horn or the ivory gate, I cannot tell. The dream is this: Let us suppose that wisdom is such as we are now defining, and that she has absolute sway over us; then each action will be done according to the arts or sciences, and no one professing to be a pilot when he is not, or any physician or general, or any one else pretending to know matters of which he is ignorant, will deceive or elude us; our health will be improved; our safety at sea, and also in battle, will be assured; our coats and shoes, and all other instruments and implements will be skilfully made, because the workmen will be good and true. Aye, and if you please, you may suppose that prophecy, which is the knowledge of the future, will be under the control of wisdom, and that she will deter deceivers and set up the true prophets in their place as the revealers of the future. Now I quite agree that mankind, thus provided, would live and act according to knowledge, for wisdom would watch and prevent ignorance from intruding on us. But whether by acting according to knowledge we shall act well and be happy, my dear Critias,--this is a point which we have not yet been able to determine.

Yet I think, he replied, that if you discard knowledge, you will hardly find the crown of happiness in anything else.

But of what is this knowledge? I said. Just answer me that small question. Do you mean a knowledge of shoemaking?

God forbid.

Or of working in brass?

Certainly not.

Or in wool, or wood, or anything of that sort?

No, I do not.

Then, I said, we are giving up the doctrine that he who lives according to knowledge is happy, for these live according to knowledge, and yet they are not allowed by you to be happy; but I think that you mean to confine happiness to particular individuals who live according to knowledge, such for example as the prophet, who, as I was saying, knows the future. Is it of him you are speaking or of some one else?

Yes, I mean him, but there are others as well.

Yes, I said, some one who knows the past and present as well as the future, and is ignorant of nothing. Let us suppose that there is such a person, and if there is, you will allow that he is the most knowing of all living men.

Certainly he is.

Yet I should like to know one thing more: which of the different kinds of knowledge makes him happy? or do all equally make him happy?

Not all equally, he replied.

But which most tends to make him happy? the knowledge of what past, present, or future thing? May I infer this to be the knowledge of the game of draughts?

Nonsense about the game of draughts.

Or of computation?

No.

Or of health?

That is nearer the truth, he said.

And that knowledge which is nearest of all, I said, is the knowledge of what?

The knowledge with which he discerns good and evil.

Monster! I said; you have been carrying me round in a circle, and all this time hiding from me the fact that the life according to knowledge is not that which makes men act rightly and be happy, not even if knowledge include all the sciences, but one science only, that of good and evil. For, let me ask you, Critias, whether, if you take away this, medicine will not equally give health, and shoemaking equally produce shoes, and the art of the weaver clothes?--whether the art of the pilot will not equally save our lives at sea, and the art of the general in war?

Quite so.

And yet, my dear Critias, none of these things will be well or beneficially done, if the science of the good be wanting.

True.

But that science is not wisdom or temperance, but a science of human advantage; not a science of other sciences, or of ignorance, but of good and evil: and if this be of use, then wisdom or temperance will not be of use.

And why, he replied, will not wisdom be of use? For, how-ever much we assume that wisdom is a science of sciences, and has a sway over other sciences, surely she will have this particular science of the good under her control, and in this way will benefit us.

And will wisdom give health? I said; is not this rather the effect of medicine? Or does wisdom do the work of any of the other arts,--do they not each of them do their own work? Have we not long ago asseverated that wisdom is only the knowledge of knowledge and of ignorance, and of nothing else?

That is obvious.

Then wisdom will not be the producer of health.

Certainly not.

The art of health is different.

Yes, different.

Nor does wisdom give advantage, my good friend; for that again we have just now been attributing to another art.

Very true.

How then can wisdom be advantageous, when giving no advantage?

That, Socrates, is certainly inconceivable.

You see then, Critias, that I was not far wrong in fearing that I could have no sound notion about wisdom; I was quite right in depreciating myself; for that which is admitted to be the best of all things would never have seemed to us useless, if I had been good for anything at an enquiry. But now I have been utterly defeated, and have failed to discover what that is to which the imposer of names gave this name of temper-ance or wisdom. And yet many more admissions were made by us than could be fairly granted; for we admitted that there was a science of science, although the argument said No, and protested against us; and we admitted further, that this science knew the works of the other sciences (although this too was denied by the argument), because we wanted to show that the wise man had knowledge of what he knew and did not know; also we nobly disregarded, and never even considered, the impossibility of a man knowing in a sort of way that which he does not know at all; for our assumption was, that he knows that which he does not know; than which nothing, as I think, can be more irrational. And yet, after finding us so easy and good-natured, the enquiry is still unable to discover the truth; but mocks us to a degree, and has gone out of its way to prove the inutility of that which we admitted only by a sort of supposition and fiction to be the true definition of temperance or wisdom: which result, as far as I am concerned, is not so much to be lamented, I said. But for your sake, Charmides, I am very sorry--that you, having such beauty and such wisdom and temperance of soul, should have no profit or good in life from your wisdom and temperance. And still more am I grieved about the charm which I learned with so much pain, and to so little profit, from the Thracian, for the sake of a thing which is nothing worth. I think indeed that there is a mistake, and that I must be a bad enquirer, for wisdom or temperance I believe to be really a great good; and happy are you, Charmides, if you certainly possess it. Wherefore examine yourself, and see whether you have this gift and can do without the charm; for if you can, I would rather advise you to regard me simply as a fool who is never able to reason out anything; and to rest assured that the more wise and temperate you are, the happier you will be.

Charmides said: I am sure that I do not know, Socrates, whether I have or have not this gift of wisdom and temperance; for how can I know whether I have a thing, of which even you and Critias are, as you say, unable to discover the nature?--(not that I believe you.) And further, I am sure, Socrates, that I do need the charm, and as far as I am concerned, I shall be willing to be charmed by you daily, until you say that I have had enough.

Very good, Charmides, said Critias; if you do this I shall have a proof of your temperance, that is, if you allow yourself to be charmed by Socrates, and never desert him at all.

You may depend on my following and not deserting him, said Charmides: if you who are my guardian command me, I should be very wrong not to obey you.

And I do command you, he said.

Then I will do as you say, and begin this very day.

You sirs, I said, what are you conspiring about?

We are not conspiring, said Charmides, we have conspired already.

And are you about to use violence, without even going through the forms of justice?

Yes, I shall use violence, he replied, since he orders me; and therefore you had better consider well.

But the time for consideration has passed, I said, when violence is employed; and you, when you are determined on anything, and in the mood of violence, are irresistible.

Do not you resist me then, he said.

I will not resist you, I replied.

Made in the USA
Monee, IL
25 August 2022

12498075R00066